TOWARD A
PSYCHOLOGY
OF BEING

Wilder Publications, Inc.
PO Box 10641
Blacksburg, VA 24063

ISBN 10: 1-61720-266-5
ISBN 13: 978-1-61720-266-7
First Edition

10 9 8 7 6 5 4 3 2 1

TOWARD A PSYCHOLOGY OF BEING

Abraham H. Maslow

Contents

Preface. 5
Acknowledgment. 9

I. A Larger Jurisdiction for Psychology

Introduction: Toward a Psychology of Health. 14
What Psychology Can Learn from the Existentialists. 19

II. Growth and Motivation

Deficiency Motivation and Growth Motivation. 26
Defense and Growth. 44
The Need to Know and the Fear of Knowing. 54

III. Growth and Cognition

Cognition of Being in the Peak-Experiences. 61
Peak-Experiences as Acute Identity-Experiences. 85
Some Dangers of Being-Cognition. 93
Resistance to Being Rubricized. 101

IV. Creativeness

Creativity in Self-Actualizing People. 106

V. Values

Psychological Data and Human Values. 115
Values, Growth, and Health. 128
Health as Transcendence of Environment. 136

VI. Future Tasks

Some Basic Propositions of a Growth and Self-Actualization Psychology. 142

Appendix A: Are Our Publications and Conventions Suitable for the
Personal Psychologies?. 161

Appendix B: Bibliography. 165

Footnotes. 174

Preface

I have had a great deal of trouble choosing a title for this book. The concept "psychological health," though still necessary, has various intrinsic shortcomings for scientific purposes which are discussed at various appropriate places in the book. So also does "psychological illness" as Szasz (160a) and the existential psychologists (110, 111) have recently stressed. We can still use these normative terms, and, as a matter of fact, for heuristic reasons we *must* use them at this time; and yet I am convinced that they will be obsolete within a decade.

A much better term is "self actualization" as I have used it. It stresses "full-humanness," the development of the biologically based nature of man, and therefore is (empirically) normative for the whole species rather than for particular times and places, i.e., it is less culturally relative. It conforms to biological destiny, rather than to historically-arbitrary, culturally-local value-models as the terms "health" and "illness" often do. It also has empirical content and operational meaning.

However, besides being clumsy from a literary point of view, this term has proven to have the unforeseen shortcomings of appearing a) to imply selfishness rather than altruism, b) to slur the aspect of duty and of dedication to life tasks, c) to neglect the ties to other people and to society, and the dependence of individual fulfillment upon a "good society,") to neglect the demand-character of non-human reality, and its intrinsic fascination and interest, e) to neglect egolessness and self-transcendence, and f) to stress, by implication, activity rather than passivity or receptivity. This has turned out to be so in spite of my careful efforts to describe the empirical *fact* that self-actualizing people are altruistic, dedicated, self-transcending, social, etc. (97, Chapter 14).

The word "self" seems to put people off, and my redefinitions and empirical description are often helpless before the powerful linguistic habit of identifying "self" with "selfish" and with pure autonomy. Also I have found to my dismay that some intelligent and capable psychologists (70, 134, 157a) persist in treating my empirical description of the characteristics of self-actualizing people as if I had arbitrarily invented these characteristics instead of discovering them.

"Full-humanness" seems to me to avoid some of these misunderstandings. And also "human diminution or stunting" serves as a better substitute for "illness" and even perhaps also for neurosis, psychosis, and psychopathy. At least these terms are more useful for general psychological and social theory if not for psychotherapeutic practice.

The terms "Being" and "Becoming" as I use them throughout this book are even better, even though they are not yet widely enough used to serve as common coin. This is a pity because the Being-psychology is certainly very different from the Becoming-psychology and the deficiency-psychology, as we shall see. I am convinced that psychologists must move in this direction of reconciling the B-psychology with the D-psychology, i.e., the perfect with the imperfect, the ideal with the actual, the eupsychian with the extant, the timeless with the temporal, end-psychology with means-psychology.

This book is a continuation of my *Motivation and Personality*, published in 1954. It was constructed in about the same way, that is, by doing one piece at a time of the larger theoretical structure. It is a predecessor to work yet to be done toward the construction of a comprehensive, systematic and empirically based general psychology and philosophy which includes both the depths and the heights of human nature. The last chapter is to some extent a program for this future work, and serves as a bridge to it. It is a first attempt to integrate the "health-and-growth psychology" with psychopathology and psychoanalytic dynamics, the dynamic with the holistic, Becoming with Being, good with evil, positive with negative. Phrased in another way, it is an effort to build on the general psychoanalytic base and on the scientific-positivistic base of experimental psychology, the Eupsychian, B-psychological and metamotivational superstructure which these two systems lack, going beyond their limits.

It is very difficult, I have found, to communicate to others my simultaneous respect for and impatience with these two comprehensive psychologies. So many people insist on being *either* pro-Freudian *or* anti-Freudian, pro-scientific-psychology *or* anti-scientific-psychology, etc. In my opinion all such loyalty-positions are silly. Our job is to integrate these various truths into the *whole* truth, which should be our only loyalty.

It is quite clear to me that scientific methods (broadly conceived) are our only ultimate ways of being sure that we *do* have truth. But here also it is too easy to misunderstand and to fall into a pro-science or anti-science dichotomy. I have already written on this subject (97, Chapters 1, 2, and 3). These are criticisms of orthodox, 19th Century scientism and I intend to continue with this enterprise, of enlarging the methods and the jurisdiction of science so as to make it more capable of taking up the tasks of the new, personal, experiential psychologies (104).

Science, as it is customarily conceived by the orthodox, is quite inadequate to these tasks. But I am certain that it need not limit itself to these orthodox ways. It need not abdicate from the problems of love, creativeness, value, beauty, imagination, ethics and joy, leaving these altogether to "non-scientists," to poets, prophets, priests, dramatists, artists, or diplomats. All of these people may have wonderful insights, ask the questions that need to be asked, put forth challenging hypotheses, and may even be correct and true much of the time. But however sure *they* may be, they can never make mankind sure. They can convince only those who already agree with them, and a few more. Science is the only way we have of shoving truth down the reluctant throat. Only science can overcome characterological differences in seeing and believing. Only science can progress.

The fact remains however that it *has* come into a kind of dead end, and (in some of its forms) *can* be seen as a threat and a danger to mankind, or at least to the highest and noblest qualities and aspirations of mankind. Many sensitive people, especially artists, are afraid that science besmirches and depresses, that it tears things apart rather than integrating them, thereby killing rather than creating.

None of this I feel is necessary. All that is needed for science to be a help in positive human fulfillment is an enlarging and deepening of the conception of its nature, its goals and its methods.

I hope the reader will not feel this credo to be inconsistent with the rather literary and philosophical tone of this book and my previous one. At any rate, I don't. The broad sketching out of a general theory requires this kind of treatment, for the time being at least. Partly also it is due to the fact that most of the chapters in this book were prepared first as lectures.

This book, like my previous one, is full of affirmations which are based on pilot researches, bits of evidence, on personal observation, on theoretical deduction and on sheer hunch. These are generally phrased so that they can be proven true or false. That is, they are hypotheses, i.e., presented for testing rather than for final belief. They are also obviously relevant and pertinent, i.e., their possible correctness or incorrectness is important to other branches of psychology. They matter. They should therefore generate research and I expect they will. For these reasons, I consider this book to be in the realm of science, or pre-science, rather than of exhortation, or of personal philosophy, or literary expression.

A word about contemporary intellectual currents in psychology may help to locate this book in its proper place. The two comprehensive theories of human nature most influencing psychology until recently have been the Freudian and the experimental-positivistic-behavioristic. All other theories were less comprehensive and their adherents formed many splinter groups. In the last few years, however, these various groups have rapidly been coalescing into a third, increasingly comprehensive theory of human nature, into what might be called a "Third Force." This group includes the Adlerians, Rankians, and Jungians, as well as all the neo-Freudians (or neo-Adlerians) and the post-Freudians (psychoanalytic ego-psychologists as well as writers like Marcuse, Wheelis, Marmor, Szasz, N. Brown, H. Lynd, and Schachtel, who are taking over from the Talmudic psychoanalysts). In addition, the influence of Kurt Goldstein and his organismic-psychology is steadily growing. So also is that of Gestalt therapy, of the Gestalt and Lewinian psychologists, of the general-semanticists, and of such personality-psychologists as G. Allport, G. Murphy, J. Moreno and H. A. Murray. A new and powerful influence is existential psychology and psychiatry. Dozens of other major contributors can be grouped as Self-psychologists, phenomenological psychologists, growth-psychologists, Rogerian psychologists, humanistic psychologists, and so on and so on and so on. A full list is impossible. A simpler way of grouping these is available in the five journals in which this group is most apt to publish, all relatively new. These are the *Journal of Individual Psychology* (University of Vermont, Burlington, Vt.), the *American Journal of Psychoanalysis* (220 W. 98th St., New York 25, N.Y.), the *Journal of Existential Psychiatry* (679 N. Michigan Ave., Chicago 11, Ill.), the *Review of Existential Psychology and Psychiatry* (Duquesne University, Pittsburgh, Pa.), and the newest one, the *Journal of Humanistic Psychology* (2637 Marshall Drive, Palo Alto, Calif). In addition, the journal Manas (P.O. Box 32,112, El Sereno Station, Los Angeles 32, Calif.) applies this point of view to the personal and social philosophy of the intelligent layman. The bibliography at the back of this book, though not complete, is a fair sampling of the writings of this group. The present book belongs in this stream of thought.

Acknowledgments

I shall not repeat here the acknowledgments already made in the preface to my *Motivation and Personality*. I wish now only to add the following.

I have been unusually fortunate in my departmental colleagues, Eugenia Hanfmann, Richard Held, Richard Jones, James Klee, Ricardo Morant, Ulric Neisser, Harry Rand, and Walter Toman, all of whom have been collaborators, sounding boards and debating partners for various parts of this book. I wish to tell them here of my affection and respect for them and to thank them for their help.

It has been my privilege for ten years to have continuing discussions with a learned, brilliant, and skeptical colleague, Dr. Frank Manuel of the Department of History at Brandeis University. I have not only enjoyed this friendship but have also been taught a great deal.

I have had a similar relationship with another friend and colleague, Dr. Harry Rand, a practicing psychoanalyst. For ten years we have continuously pursued together the deeper meanings of the Freudian theories, and one product of this collaboration has already been published (103). Neither Dr. Manuel nor Dr. Rand agrees with my general slant nor does Walter Toman, also a psychoanalyst, with whom I have also had many discussions and debates. Perhaps for that very reason they have helped me to sharpen my own conclusions.

Dr. Ricardo Morant and I collaborated in seminars, experiments, and in various writings. This has helped to keep me closer to the mainstream of experimental psychology. My Chapters 3 and 6 especially owe much to the help of Dr. James Klee.

The sharp but amicable debates in the Graduate Colloquium of our Department of Psychology with these and my other colleagues, and with our graduate students, have been continuously instructive. So also have I learned much from daily formal and informal contacts with many members of the Brandeis faculty and staff, as learned, sophisticated and argumentative a group of intellectuals as exists any place.

I learned much from my colleagues of the Values Symposium held at MIT (102) especially Frank Bowditch, Robert Hartman, Gyorgy Kepes, Dorothy Lee, and Walter Weisskopf. Adrian van Kaam, Rollo May, and James Klee introduced me to the literature of existentialism. Frances Wilson Schwartz (179, 180) taught me first about creative art education and its many implications for growth-psychology. Aldous Huxley (68a) was among the first to convince me that I had better be serious about the psychology of religion and mysticism. Felix Deutsch helped me to learn about psychoanalysis from the inside, by experiencing it. My intellectual indebtedness to Kurt Goldstein is so great that I have dedicated this book to him.

Much of this book was written during a sabbatical year which I owe to enlightened administrative policy at my University. I wish also to thank the Ella Lyman Cabot Trust for a grant that helped free me from thinking about money during this year of writing. It is very difficult to do sustained theoretical work during the ordinary academic year.

Miss Verna Collette has done most of the typing for this book. I wish to thank her for her unusual helpfulness, patience, and hard work for which I am extremely grateful. I owe thanks for secretarial help also to Gwen Whately, Lorraine Kaufman and Sandy Mazer.

Chapter 1 is a revised version of a portion of a lecture given at the Cooper Union, New York City, October 18, 1954. The full text was published in *Self*, edited by Clark Moustakas, Harper & Bros., 1956, and is used here with the permission of the publisher. It has also been reprinted in J. Coleman, F. Libaw, and W. Martinson, *Success in College.* Scott, Foresman, 1961.

Chapter 2 is a revised version of a paper read before a Symposium on Existential Psychology, at the 1959 Convention of The American Psychological Association. It was first published in *Existentialist Inquiries*, 1960, 1, 1-5, and is used here with the permission of the editor. It has since been reprinted in *Existential Psychology*, Rollo May (ed.), Random House, 1961, and in *Religious Inquiry*, 1960, No. 28, 4-7.

Chapter 3 is a condensed version of a lecture presented before the University of Nebraska Symposium on Motivation, January 13, 1955, and printed in the *Nebraska Symposium on Motivation*, 1955. M. R. Jones (ed.), University of Nebraska Press, 1955. It is used here with the permission of the publisher. It has also been reprinted in the *General Semantics Bulletin*, 1956, Nos. 18 and 19, 32-42, and in J. Coleman, *Personality Dynamics and Effective Behavior*, Scott, Foresman, 1960.

Chapter 4 was originally a lecture given before the Merrill-Palmer School Conference on Growth, May 10, 1956. It was published in the *Merrill-Palmer Quarterly*, 1956, 3, 36-47, and is used here with the permission of the editor.

Chapter 5 is a revision of the second portion of a lecture delivered at Tufts University which will be published in toto in *The Journal of General Psychology* in 1963. It is used here with the permission of the editor. The first half of the lecture summarizes all the evidence available to justify postulating an instinctoid need to know.

Chapter 6 is a revised version of a presidential address before the Division of Personality and Social Psychology, American Psychological Association, September 1, 1956. It was published in the *Journal of Genetic Psychology*, 1959, 94, 43-66, and is used here with the permission of the editor. It was reprinted in *International Journal of Parapsychology*, 1960, 2, 23-54.

Chapter 7 is a revised version of a lecture first read before a Karen Horney Memorial Meeting on Identity and Alienation, Association for the Advancement of Psychoanalysis, New York City, October 5, 1960. Published in *American Journal of Psychoanalysis*, 1961, 21, 254. It is used here with the permission of the editors.

Chapter 8 was first published in the Kurt Goldstein number of the *Journal of Individual Psychology*, 1959, 15, 24-32, and is reprinted here with the permission of the editors.

Chapter 9 is a revised version of a paper first published in *Perspectives in Psychological Theory*. B. Kaplan and S. Wapner (eds.), International Universities Press, 1960, a collection of essays in honor of Heinz Werner. It is used here with the permission of the editors and the publisher.

Chapter 10 is a revised version of a lecture delivered February 28, 1959, Michigan State University, East Lansing, Michigan, as one of a series on Creativeness. This series has been published as *Creativity and Its Cultivation*, H. H. Anderson (ed.), Harper & Bros., 1959. The lecture is used here with the permission of the editor and the publishers. It has been reprinted in *Electro-Mechanical Design*, 1959 (Jan. and Aug. numbers), and in *General Semantics Bulletin*, 1959-60, Nos. 23 and 24, 45-50.

Chapter 11 is a revision and expansion of a lecture given before the Conference on New Knowledge in Human Values, October 4, 1957, Massachusetts Institute of Technology, Cambridge, Mass. Printed in *New Knowledge in Human Values*, A. H. Maslow (ed.), Harper & Bros., 1958, and used here by permission of the publishers.

Chapter 12 is a revised and expanded version of a lecture read before a Symposium on Values, Academy of Psychoanalysis, New York City, December 10, 1960.

Chapter 13 was a lecture before a Symposium on Research Implications of Positive Mental Health, Eastern Psychological Association, April 15, 1960. Printed in *Journal of Humanistic Psychology*, 1961, 1, 1-7, and used here with the permission of the editor.

Chapter 14 is a revised and enlarged version of a paper written in 1958 for ASCD, *Perceiving, Behaving, Becoming: A New Focus for Education*, A. Combs (ed.), 1962 Yearbook of the Association for Supervision and Curriculum

Development, Washington, D.C., 1962. In part, these propositions are a summary of the whole of this book and my previous one. Partly also it is a programmatic extrapolation into the future.

A. H. M.

A Larger Jurisdiction for Psychology

Introduction: Toward a Psychology of Health

There is now emerging over the horizon a new conception of human sickness and of human health, a psychology that I find so thrilling and so full of wonderful possibilities that I yield to the temptation to present it publicly even before it is checked and confirmed, and before it can be called reliable scientific knowledge.

The basic assumptions of this point of view are:

1. We have, each of us, an essential biologically based inner nature, which is to some degree "natural," intrinsic, given, and, in a certain limited sense, unchangeable, or, at least, unchanging.

2. Each person's inner nature is in part unique to himself and in part species-wide.

3. It is possible to study this inner nature scientifically and to discover what it is like—(not *invent*—*discover*).

4. This inner nature, as much as we know of it so far, seems not to be intrinsically evil, but rather either neutral or positively "good." What we call evil behavior appears most often to be a secondary reaction to frustration of this intrinsic nature.

5. Since this inner nature is good or neutral rather than bad, it is best to bring it out and to encourage it rather than to suppress it. If it is permitted to guide our life, we grow healthy, fruitful, and happy.

6. If this essential core of the person is denied or suppressed, he gets sick sometimes in obvious ways, sometimes in subtle ways, sometimes immediately, sometimes later.

7. This inner nature is not strong and overpowering and unmistakable like the instincts of animals. It is weak and delicate and subtle and easily overcome by habit, cultural pressure, and wrong attitudes toward it.

8. Even though weak, it rarely disappears in the normal person—perhaps not even in the sick person. Even though denied, it persists underground forever pressing for actualization.

9. Somehow, these conclusions must all be articulated with the necessity of discipline, deprivation, frustration, pain, and tragedy. To the extent that these experiences reveal and foster and fulfill our inner nature, to that extent they are desirable experiences.

Observe that if these assumptions are proven true, they promise a scientific ethics, a natural value system, a court of ultimate appeal for the determination of good and bad, of right and wrong. The more we learn about man's natural tendencies, the easier it will be to tell him how to be good, how to be happy, how to be fruitful, how to respect himself, how to love, how to fulfill his highest potentialities. This amounts to automatic solution of many of the personality problems of the future. The thing to do seems to be to find out what you are *really* like inside, deep down, as a member of the human species and as a particular individual.

The study of such healthy people can teach us much about our own mistakes, our shortcomings, the proper directions in which to grow. Every age but ours has had its model, its ideal. All of these have been given up by our culture; the saint, the hero, the gentleman, the knight, the mystic. About all we have left is the well-adjusted man without problems, a very pale and doubtful substitute. Perhaps we shall soon be able to use as our guide and model the fully growing and self-fulfilling human being, the one in whom all his potentialities are coming to full development, the one whose inner nature expresses itself freely, rather than being warped, suppressed, or denied.

The serious thing for each person to recognize vividly and poignantly, each for himself, is that every falling away from species-virtue, every crime against one's own nature, every evil act, *every one without exception records itself* in our unconscious and makes us despise ourselves. Karen Horney had a good word to describe this unconscious perceiving and remembering; she said it "registers." If we do something we are ashamed of, it "registers" to our discredit, and if we do something honest or fine or good, it "registers" to our credit. The net results ultimately are either one or the other—either we respect and accept ourselves or we despise ourselves and feel contemptible, worthless, and unlovable. Theologians used to use the word *"accidie"* to describe the sin of failing to do with one's life all that one knows one could do.

This point of view in no way denies the usual Freudian picture. But it does add to it and supplement it. To oversimplify the matter somewhat, it is as if Freud supplied to us the sick half of psychology and we must now fill it out with the healthy half. Perhaps this health psychology will give us more possibility for controlling and improving our lives and for making ourselves better people. Perhaps this will be more fruitful than asking "how to get *unsick.*"

How can we encourage free development? What are the best educational conditions for it? Sexual? Economic? Political? What kind of world do we need for such people to grow in? What kind of world will such people create? Sick people are made by a sick culture; healthy people are made possible by a healthy culture. But it is just as true that sick individuals make their culture more sick and that healthy individuals make their culture more healthy. Improving individual health is one approach to making a better world. To express it in another way, encouragement of personal growth is a real possibility; cure of actual neurotic symptoms is far less possible without outside help. It is relatively easy to try deliberately to make oneself a more honest man; it is very difficult to try to cure one's own compulsions or obsessions.

The classical approach to personality problems considers them to be problems in an undesirable sense. Struggle, conflict, guilt, bad conscience, anxiety, depression, frustration, tension, shame, self-punishment, feeling of inferiority or unworthiness—they all cause psychic pain, they disturb efficiency of performance, and they are uncontrollable. They are therefore automatically regarded as sick and undesirable and they get "cured" away as soon as possible.

But all of these symptoms are found also in healthy people, or in people who are growing toward health. Supposing you *should* feel guilty and don't? Supposing you have attained a nice stabilization of forces and you *are* adjusted? Perhaps adjustment and stabilization, while good because it cuts your pain, is also bad because development toward a higher ideal ceases?

Erich Fromm, in a very important book (50), attacked the classical Freudian notion of a superego because this concept was entirely authoritarian and relativistic. That is to say, your superego or your conscience was supposed by Freud to be primarily the internalization of the wishes, demands, and ideals of the father and mother, whoever they happen to be. But supposing they are criminals? Then what kind of conscience do you have? Or supposing you have a rigid moralizing father who hates fun? Or a psychopath? This conscience exists—Freud was right. We do get our ideals largely from such early figures and not from Sunday School books read later in life. But there is also another element in conscience, or, if you like, another kind of conscience, which we all have either weakly or strongly. And this is the "intrinsic conscience." This is based upon the unconscious and preconscious perception of our own nature, of our own destiny, or our own capacities, of our own "call" in life. It insists that we be true to our inner nature and that we do not deny it out of weakness or for advantage or for any other reason. He who belies his talent, the born painter who sells stockings instead, the intelligent man who lives a stupid life, the man who sees the truth and keeps his mouth shut, the coward who gives up his manliness, all these people perceive in a deep way that they have done wrong to themselves and despise themselves for it. Out of this self-punishment may come only neurosis, but there may equally well come renewed courage, righteous indignation, increased self-respect, because of thereafter doing the right thing; in a word, growth and improvement can come through pain and conflict.

In essence I am deliberately rejecting our present easy distinction between sickness and health, at least as far as surface symptoms are concerned. Does sickness mean having symptoms? I maintain now that sickness might consist of *not* having symptoms when you should. Does health mean being symptom-free? I deny it. Which of the Nazis at Auschwitz or Dachau were healthy? Those with stricken conscience or those with a nice, clear, happy conscience? Was it possible for a profoundly human person not to feel conflict, suffering, depression, rage, etc?

In a word if you tell me you have a personality problem I am not certain until I know you better whether to say "Good!" or "I'm sorry." It depends on the reasons. And these, it seems, may be bad reasons, or they may be good reasons.

An example is the changing attitude of psychologists toward popularity, toward adjustment, even toward delinquency. Popular with whom? Perhaps it is better for a youngster to be *unpopular* with the neighboring snobs or with the local country club set. Adjusted to what? To a bad culture? To a dominating parent? What shall we think of a well-adjusted slave? A well-adjusted prisoner? Even the behavior problem boy is being looked upon with new tolerance. *Why* is he delinquent? Most often it is for sick reasons. But occasionally it is for good reasons and the boy is simply resisting exploitation, domination, neglect, contempt, and trampling upon.

Clearly what will be called personality problems depends on who is doing the calling. The slave owner? The dictator? The patriarchal father? The husband who wants his wife to remain a child? It seems quite clear that personality problems may sometimes be loud protests against the crushing of one's psychological bones, of one's true inner nature. What is sick then is *not* to protest while this crime is being committed. And I am sorry to report my impression that most people do not protest under such treatment. They take it and pay years later, in neurotic and psychosomatic symptoms of various kinds, or perhaps in some cases never become aware that they are sick, that they have missed true happiness, true fulfillment of promise, a rich emotional life, and a serene, fruitful old age, that they have never known how wonderful it is to be creative, to react aesthetically, to find life thrilling.

The question of desirable grief and pain or the necessity for it must also be faced. Is growth and self-fulfillment possible at all without pain and grief and sorrow and turmoil? If these are to some extent necessary and unavoidable, then to what extent? If grief and pain are sometimes necessary for growth of the person, then we must learn not to protect people from them automatically as if they were always bad. Sometimes they may be good and desirable in view of the ultimate good consequences. Not allowing people to go through their pain, and protecting them from it, may turn out to be a kind of over-protection, which in turn implies a certain lack of respect for the integrity and the intrinsic nature and the future development of the individual.

What Psychology Can Learn from the Existentialists

If we study existentialism from the point of view of "What's in it for the psychologist?" we find much that is too vague and too difficult to understand from a scientific point of view (not confirmable or disconfirmable). But we also find a great deal that is of profit. From such a point of view, we find it to be not so much a totally new revelation, as a stressing, confirming, sharpening and rediscovering of trends already existing in "Third Force psychology."

To me existential psychology means essentially two main emphases. First, it is a radical stress on the concept of identity and the experience of identity as a *sine qua non* of human nature and of any philosophy or science of human nature. I choose this concept as *the* basic one partly because I understand it better than terms like essence, existence, ontology and so on, and partly because I feel also that it can be worked with empirically, if not now, then soon.

But then a paradox results, for the American psychologists have *also* been impressed with the quest for identity. (Allport, Rogers, Goldstein, Fromm, Wheelis, Erikson, Murray, Murphy, Horney, May, et al). And I must say that these writers are a lot clearer and a lot closer to raw fact; i.e., more empirical than are, e.g., the Germans, Heidegger, Jaspers.

Secondly, it lays great stress on starting from experiential knowledge rather than from systems of concepts or abstract categories or a prioris. Existentialism rests on phenomenology, i.e., it uses personal, subjective experience as the foundation upon which abstract knowledge is built.

But many psychologists also have started with this same stress, not to mention all the various brands of psychoanalysts.

1. Conclusion number 1 is, then, that European philosophers and American psychologists are not so far apart as appears at first. We Americans have been "talking prose all the time and didn't know it." Partly of course this simultaneous development in different countries is itself an indication that the people who have independently been coming to the same conclusions are all responding to something real outside themselves.

2. This something real I believe is the total collapse of all sources of values outside the individual. Many European existentialists are largely reacting to Nietzsche's conclusion that God is dead, and perhaps to the fact that Marx also is dead. The Americans have learned that political democracy and economic prosperity don't in themselves solve any of the basic value problems. There's no

place else to turn but inward, to the self, as the locus of values. Paradoxically, even some of the religious existentialists will go along with this conclusion part of the way.

3. It is extremely important for psychologists that the existentialists may supply psychology with the underlying philosophy which it now lacks. Logical positivism has been a failure, especially for clinical and personality psychologists. At any rate, the basic philosophical problems will surely be opened up for discussion again and perhaps psychologists will stop relying on pseudo-solutions or on unconscious, unexamined philosophies they picked up as children.

4. An alternative phrasing of the core (for us Americans) of European existentialism is that it deals radically with that human predicament presented by the gap between human aspirations and human limitations (between what the human being *is*, what he would *like* to be, and what he *could* be). This is not so far off from the identity problem as it might sound at first. A person is both actuality *and* potentiality.

That serious concern with this discrepancy could revolutionize psychology, there is no doubt in my mind. Various literatures already support such a conclusion, e.g., projective testing, self-actualization, the various peakexperiences (in which this gap is bridged), the Jungian psychologies, various theological thinkers, etc.

Not only this, but they raise also the problems and techniques of integration of this twofold nature of man, his lower and his higher, his creatureliness and his god-likeness. On the whole, most philosophies and religions, Eastern as well as Western, have dichotomized them, teaching that the way to become "higher" is to renounce and master "the lower." The existentialists, however, teach that *both axe* simultaneously defining characteristics of human nature. Neither can be repudiated; they can only be integrated.

But we already know something of these integration techniques—of insight, of intellect in the broader sense, of love, of creativeness, of humor and tragedy, of play, of art. I suspect we will focus our studies on these integrative techniques more than we have in the past.

Another consequence for my thinking of this stress on the twofold nature of man is the realization that some problems must remain eternally insoluble.

5. From this flows naturally a concern with the ideal, authentic, or perfect or godlike human being, a study of human potentialities as *now* existing in a certain sense, as *current* knowable reality. This, too, may sound merely literary but it's not. I remind you that this is just a fancy way of asking the old,

unanswered questions, "What are the goals of therapy, of education, of bringing up children?"

It also implies another truth and another problem which calls urgently for attention. Practically every serious description of the 'authentic person' extant implies that such a person, by virtue of what he has become, assumes a new relation to his society and indeed, to society in general. He not only transcends himself in various ways; he also transcends his culture. He resists enculturation. He becomes more detached from his culture and from his society. He becomes a little more a member of his species and a little less a member of his local group. My feeling is that most sociologists and anthropologists will take this hard. I therefore confidently expect controversy in this area.

6. From the European writers, we can and should pick up their greater emphasis on what they call "philosophical anthropology," that is, the attempt to define man, and the differences between man and any other species, between man and objects, and between man and robots. What are his unique and defining characteristics? What is so essential to man that without it he would no longer be defined as a man?

On the whole this is a task from which American psychology has abdicated. The various behaviorisms don't generate any such definition, at least none that can be taken seriously (what *would* an S-R man be like? And who would like to be one?) Freud's picture of man was clearly unsuitable, leaving out as it did his aspirations, his realizable hopes, his godlike qualities. The fact that Freud supplied us with our most comprehensive systems of psychopathology and psychotherapy is beside the point as the contemporary ego-psychologists are finding out.

7. The Europeans are stressing the self-making of the self, in a way that the Americans don't. Both the Freudians and the self-actualization and growth theorists in this country talk more about *discovering* the self (as if it were there waiting to be found) and of *uncovering* therapy (shovel away the top layers and you'll see what has been always lying there, hidden). To say, however, that the self is a project and is *altogether* created by the continual choices of the person himself, is an extreme overstatement in view of what we know of, e.g., the constitutional and genetic determinants of personality. This clash of opinion is a problem that can be settled empirically.

8. A problem we psychologists have been ducking is the problem of responsibility, and, necessarily tied in with it, the concepts of courage and of will in the personality. Perhaps this is close to what the psychoanalysts are now calling "ego strength."

9. American psychologists have listened to Allport's call for an idiographic psychology but haven't done much about it. Not even the clinical psychologists have. We now have an added push from the phenomenologists and existentialists in this direction, one that will be *very* hard to resist, indeed I think, theoretically *impossible* to resist. If the study of the uniqueness of the individual does not fit into what we know of science, then so much the worse for that conception of science. It, too, will have to endure re-creation.

10. Phenomenology has a history in American psychological thinking (87), but on the whole I think it has languished. The European phenomenologists with their excruciatingly careful and laborious demonstrations, can reteach us that the best way of understanding another human being, or at least *a* way necessary for some purposes, is to get into *his* Weltanschauung and to be able to see *his* world through *his* eves. Of course such a conclusion is rough on any positivistic philosophy of science.

11. The existentialist stress on the ultimate aloneness of the individual is a useful reminder for us, not only to work out further the concepts of decision, of responsibility, of choice, of self-creation, of autonomy, of identity itself. It also makes more problematic and more fascinating the mystery of communication between alonenesses via, e.g., intuition and empathy, love and altruism, identification with others, and homonomy in general. We take these for granted. It would be better if we regarded them as miracles to be explained.

12. Another preoccupation of existentialist writers can be phrased very simply, I think. It is the dimension of seriousness and profundity of living (or perhaps the "tragic sense of life") contrasted with the shallow and superficial life, which is a kind of diminished living, a defense against the ultimate problems of life. This is not just a literary concept. It has real operational meaning, for instance, in psychotherapy. I (and others) have been increasingly impressed with the fact that tragedy can sometimes be therapeutic, and that therapy often seems to work best when people are *driven* into it by pain. It is when the shallow life doesn't work that it is questioned and that there occurs a call to fundamentals. Shallowness in psychology doesn't work either as the existentialists are demonstrating very clearly.

13. The existentialists along with many other groups are helping to teach us about the limits of verbal, analytic, conceptual rationality. They are part of the current call back to raw experience as prior to any concepts or abstractions. This amounts to what I believe to be a justified critique of the whole way of thinking of the western world in the 20th century, including orthodox positivistic science and philosophy, both of which badly need re-examination.

14. Possibly most important of all the changes to be wrought by the phenomenologists and existentialists is an overdue revolution in the theory of science. I shouldn't say "wrought by" but rather "helped along by," because there are many other forces helping to destroy official philosophy of science or "scientism." It is not only the Cartesian split between subject and object that needs to be overcome. There are other radical changes made necessary by the inclusion of the psyche and of raw experience in reality, and such a change will affect not only the science of psychology but all other sciences as well, e.g., parsimony, simplicity, precision, orderliness, logic, elegance, definition, etc. are all of the realm of abstraction.

15. I close with the stimulus that has most powerfully affected me in the existentialist literature, namely, the problem of future time in psychology. Not that this, like all the other problems or pushes I have mentioned up to this point, was totally unfamiliar to me nor, I imagine, to *any* serious student of the theory of personality. The writings of Charlotte Buhler, Gordon Allport, and Kurt Goldstein should also have sensitized us to the necessity of grappling with and systematizing the dynamic role of the future in the presently existing personality, e.g., growth and becoming and possibility necessarily point toward the future; so do the concepts of potentiality and hoping, and of wishing and imagining; reduction to the concrete is a loss of future; threat and apprehension point to the future (no future = no neurosis); self-actualization is meaningless without reference to a currently active future; life can be a gestalt in time, etc., etc.

And yet the *basic and central* importance of this problem for the existentialists has something to teach us, e.g., Erwin Strauss' paper in the May volume (110). I think it fair to say that no theory of psychology will ever be complete which does not centrally incorporate the concept that man has his future within him, dynamically active at this present moment. In this sense the future can be treated as a-historical in Kurt Lewin's sense. Also we must realize that *only* the future is *in principle* unknown and unknowable, which means that all habits, defenses and coping mechanisms are doubtful and ambiguous since they are based on past experience. Only the flexibly creative person can really manage future, *only* the one who can face novelty with confidence and without fear. I am convinced that much of what we now call psychology is the study of the tricks we use to avoid the anxiety of absolute novelty by making believe the future will be like the past.

Conclusion

These considerations support my hope that we are witnessing an expansion of psychology, not a new "ism" that could turn into an antipsychology or into an antiscience.

It is possible that existentialism will not only enrich psychology. It may also be an additional push toward the establishment of another *branch* of psychology, the psychology of the fully evolved and authentic Self and its ways of being. Sutich has suggested calling this ontopsychology.

Certainly it seems more and more clear that what we call "normal" in psychology is really a psychopathology of the average, so undramatic and so widely spread that we don't even notice it ordinarily. The existentialist's study of the authentic person and of authentic living helps to throw this general phoniness, this living by illusions and by fear into a harsh, clear light which reveals it clearly as sickness, even tho widely shared.

I don't think we need take too seriously the European existentialists' exclusive harping on dread, on anguish, on despair and the like, for which their only remedy seems to be to keep a stiff upper lip. This high I.Q. whimpering on a cosmic scale occurs whenever an external source of values fails to work. They should have learned from the psychotherapists that the loss of illusions and the discovery of identity, though painful at first, can be ultimately exhilarating and strengthening.

Part II

Growth and Motivation

Deficiency Motivation and Growth Motivation

The concept "basic need" can be defined in terms of the questions which it answers and the operations which uncovered it (97). My original question was about psychopathogenesis. "What makes people neurotic?" My answer (a modification of and, I think, an improvement upon the analytic one) was, in brief, that neurosis seemed at its core, and in its beginning, to be a deficiency disease; that it was born out of being deprived of certain satisfactions which I called needs in the same sense that water and amino acids and calcium are needs, namely that their absence produces illness. Most neuroses involved, along with other complex determinants, ungratified wishes for safety, for belongingness and identification, for close love relationships and for respect and prestige. My "data" were gathered through twelve years of psychotherapeutic work and research and twenty years of personality study. One obvious control research (done at the same time and in the same operation) was on the effect of replacement therapy which showed, with many complexities, that when these deficiencies were eliminated, sicknesses tended to disappear. Still another necessary long-time control research was on the family backgrounds of both neurotic and healthy people establishing, as many others have also done, that people who are later healthy are not deprived of these essential basic-need-satisfactions, i.e., the prophylactic control (97, Chapter 5).

These conclusions, which are now in effect shared by most clinicians, therapists, and child psychologists (many of them would not phrase it as I have) make it more possible year by year to define need, in a natural, easy, spontaneous way, as a generalization of actual experiential data (rather than by fiat, arbitrarily and prematurely, *prior* to the accumulation of knowledge rather than subsequent to it (141) simply for the sake of greater objectivity).

The long-run deficiency characteristics are then the following. It is a basic or instinctoid need if

1. its absence breeds illness,

2. its presence prevents illness,

3. its restoration cures illness, under certain (very complex) free choice situations, it is preferred by the deprived person over other satisfactions,

5. it is found to be inactive, at a low ebb, or functionally absent in the healthy person.

Two additional characteristics are subjective ones, namely, conscious or unconscious yearning and desire, and feeling of lack or deficiency, as of something missing on the one hand, and, on the other, palatability. ("It tastes good.")

One last word on definition. Many of the problems that have plagued writers in this area, as they attempted to define and delimit motivation, are a consequence of the exclusive demand for behavioral, externally observable criteria. The original criterion of motivation and the one that is still used by all human beings except behavioral psychologists is the subjective one. I am motivated when I feel desire or want or yearning or wish or lack. No objectively observable state has yet been found that correlates decently with these subjective reports, i.e., no good behavioral definition of motivation has yet been found.

Now of course we ought to keep on seeking for objective correlates or indicators of subjective states. On the day when we discover such a public and external indicator of pleasure or of anxiety or of desire, psychology will have jumped forward by a century. But *until* we find it we ought not make believe that we have. Nor ought we neglect the subjective data that we do have. It is unfortunate that we cannot ask a rat to give subjective reports. Fortunately, however, we *can* ask the human being, and there is no reason in the world why we should refrain from doing so until we have a better source of data.

It is these needs which are essentially deficits in the organism, empty holes, so to speak, which must be filled up for health's sake, and furthermore must be filled from without by human beings *other* than the subject, that I shall call deficits or deficiency needs for purposes of this exposition and to set them in contrast to another and very different kind of motivation.

It would not occur to anyone to question the statement that we "need" iodine or vitamin C. I remind you that the evidence that we "need" love is of exactly the same type.

In recent years more and more psychologists have found themselves compelled to postulate some tendency to growth or self-perfection to supplement the concepts of equilibrium, homeostasis, tension-reduction, defense and other conserving motivations. This was so for various reasons.

1. *Psychotherapy.* The pressure toward health makes therapy possible. It is an absolute *sine qua non.* If there were no such trend, therapy would be inexplicable to the extent that it goes beyond the building of defenses against pain and anxiety (6, 142, 50, 67).

2. *Brain-injured soldiers.* Goldstein's work (55) is well known to all. He found it necessary to invent the concept of self-actualization to explain the reorganization of the person's capacities after injury.

3. *Psychoanalysis.* Some analysts, notably Fromm (50) and Horney (67), have found it impossible to understand even neuroses unless one postulates that they are a distorted version of an impulse toward growth, toward perfection of development, toward the fulfillment of the person's possibilities.

4. *Creativeness.* Much light is being thrown on the general subject of creativeness by the study of healthy growing and grown people, especially when contrasted with sick people. Especially does the theory of art and art education call for a concept of growth and spontaneity. (179, 180).

5. *Child Psychology.* Observation of children shows more and more clearly that healthy children *enjoy* growing and moving forward, gaining new skills, capacities and powers. This is in flat contradiction to that version of Freudian theory which conceives of every child as hanging on desperately to each adjustment that it achieves and to each state of rest or equilibrium. According to this theory, the reluctant and conservative child has continually to be kicked upstairs, out of its comfortable, preferred state of rest *into* a new frightening situation.

While this Freudian conception is continually confirmed by clinicians as largely true for insecure and frightened children, and while it is partially true for all human beings, in the main it is *untrue* for healthy, happy, secure children. In these children we see clearly an eagerness to grow up, to mature, to drop the old adjustment as outworn, like an old pair of shoes. We see in them with special clarity not only the eagerness for the new skill but also the most obvious delight in repeatedly enjoying it, the so-called *Funktionslust* of Karl Buhler (24).

For the writers in these various groups, notably Fromm (50), Horney (67), Jung (73), C. Buhler (22), Angyal (6), Rogers (143), and G. Allport (2), Schachtel (147), and Lynd (92), and recently some Catholic psychologists (9, 128), growth, individuation, autonomy, self-actualization, self-development, productiveness, self-realization, are all crudely synonymous, designating a vaguely perceived area rather than a sharply defined concept. In my opinion, it is *not* possible to define this area sharply at the present time. Nor is this desirable either, since a definition which does not emerge easily and naturally from well-known facts is apt to be inhibiting and distorting rather than helpful, since it is quite likely to be wrong or mistaken if made by an act of the will, on a priori grounds. We just don't know enough about growth yet to be able to define it well.

Its meaning can be *indicated* rather than defined, partly by positive pointing, partly by negative contrast, i.e., what is *not*. For example, it is not the same as equilibrium, homeostasis, tension-reduction, etc.

Its necessity has presented itself to its proponents partly because of dissatisfaction (certain newly noticed phenomena simply were not covered by extant theories); partly by positive needs for theories and concepts which would better serve the new humanistic value systems emerging from the breakdown of the older value systems. This present treatment, however, derives mostly from a direct study of psychologically healthy individuals. This was undertaken not only for reasons of intrinsic and personal interest but also to supply a firmer foundation for the theory of therapy, of pathology and therefore of values. The true goals of education, of family training, of psychotherapy, of self-development, it seems to me, can be discovered only by such a direct attack. The end product of growth teaches us much about the processes of growth. In a recent book (97), I have described what was learned from this study and in addition theorized very freely about various possible consequences for general psychology of this kind of direct study of good rather than bad human beings, of healthy rather than sick people, of the positive as well as the negative. (I must warn you that the data cannot be considered reliable until someone else repeats the study. The possibilities of projection are very real in such a study and of course are unlikely to be detected by the investigator himself.) I want now to discuss some of the differences that I have observed to exist between the motivational lives of healthy people and of others, i.e., people motivated by growth needs contrasted with those motivated by the basic needs.

So far as motivational status is concerned, healthy people have sufficiently gratified their basic needs for safety, belongingness, love, respect and self-esteem so that they are motivated primarily by trends to self-actualization (defined as ongoing actualization of potentials, capacities and talents, as fulfillment of mission (or call, fate, destiny, or vocation), as a fuller knowledge of, and acceptance of, the person's own intrinsic nature, as an unceasing trend toward unity, integration or synergy within the person).

Much to be preferred to this generalized definition would be a descriptive and operational one which I have already published (97). These healthy people are there defined by describing their clinically observed characteristics. These are:

1. Superior perception of reality.
2. Increased acceptance of self, of others and of nature.
3. Increased spontaneity.
4. Increase in problem-centering.
5. Increased detachment and desire for privacy.

6. Increased autonomy, and resistance to enculturation.
7. Greater freshness of appreciation, and richness of emotional reaction.
8. Higher frequency of peak experiences.
9. Increased identification with the human species.
10. Changed (the clinician would say, improved) interpersonal relations.
11. More democratic character structure.
12. Greatly increased creativeness.
13. Certain changes in the value system.

Furthermore, in this book are described also the limitations imposed upon the definition by unavoidable shortcomings in sampling and in availability of data.

One major difficulty with this conception as so far presented is its somewhat static character. Self-actualization, since I have found it only in older people, tends to be seen as an ultimate or final state of affairs, a far goal, rather than a dynamic process, active throughout life, Being, rather than Becoming.

If we define growth as the various processes which bring the person toward ultimate self-actualization, then this conforms better with the observed fact that it is going on *all* the time in the life history. It discourages also the stepwise, *all* or none, saltatory conception of motivational progression toward self-actualization in which the basic needs are completely gratified, one by one, before the next higher one emerges into consciousness. Growth is seen then not only as progressive gratification of basic needs to the point where they "disappear," but also in the form of specific growth motivations over and above these basic needs, e.g., talents, capacities, creative tendencies, constitutional potentialities. We are thereby helped also to realize that basic needs and self-actualization do not contradict each other any more than do childhood and maturity. One passes into the other and is a necessary prerequisite for it.

The differentiation between these growth-needs and basic needs which we shall explore here is a consequence of the clinical perception of qualitative differences between the motivational lives of self-actualizers and of other people. These differences, listed below, are fairly well though not perfectly described by the names deficiency-needs and growth-needs. For instance, not all physiological needs are deficits, e.g., sex, elimination, sleep and rest.

At a higher level, needs for safety, belongingness, love and respect are all clearly deficits. But the need for self-respect is a doubtful case. While the cognitive needs for curiosity-satisfaction and for a system of explanation can easily be considered deficits to be satisfied, as can also the hypothetical need for beauty, the need to create is another matter, as is also the need to express.

Apparently not all basic needs are deficits but the needs whose frustration is pathogenic are deficits. (Clearly also the sensory satisfactions that Murphy (122) has emphasized can not be considered deficits, perhaps not even needs at all.)

In any case, the psychological life of the person, in many of its aspects, is lived out differently when he is deficiency-need-gratification-bent and when he is growth-dominated or "metamotivated" or growth-motivated or self-actualizing. The following differences make this clear.

1. Attitude Toward Impulse: Impulse-Rejection and Impulse-Acceptance

Practically all historical and contemporary theories of motivation unite in regarding needs, drives and motivating states in general as annoying, irritating, unpleasant, undesirable, as something to get rid of. Motivated behavior, goal seeking, consummatory responses are all techniques for reducing these discomforts. This attitude is very explicitly assumed in such widely used descriptions of motivation as need reduction, tension reduction, drive reduction, and anxiety reduction.

This approach is understandable in animal psychology and in the behaviorism which is so heavily based upon work with animals. It may be that animals have *only* deficiency needs. Whether or not this turns out to be so, in any case we have treated animals *as if* this were so for the sake of objectivity. A goal object has to be something outside the animal organism so that we can measure the effort put out by the animal in achieving this goal.

It is also understandable that the Freudian psychology should be built upon the same attitude toward motivation that impulses are dangerous and to be fought. After all, this whole psychology is based upon experience with sick people, people who in fact suffer from bad experiences with their needs, and with their gratifications and frustrations. It is no wonder that such people should fear or even loathe their impulses which have made so much trouble for them and which they handle so badly, and that a usual way of handling them is repression.

This derogation of desire and need has, of course, been a constant theme throughout the history of philosophy, theology and psychology. The Stoics, most hedonists, practically all theologians, many political philosophers and most economic theorists have united in affirming the fact that good or happiness or pleasure is essentially the consequence of amelioration of this unpleasant state-of-affairs of wanting, of desiring, of needing.

To put it as succinctly as possible, these people all find desire or impulse to be a nuisance or even a threat and therefore will try generally to get rid of it, to deny it or to avoid it.

This contention is sometimes an accurate report of what is the case. The physiological needs, the needs for safety, for love, for respect, for information are in fact often nuisances for many people, psychic troublemakers, and problem-creators, especially for those who have had unsuccessful experiences at gratifying them and for those who cannot now count on gratification.

Even with these deficiencies, however, the case is very badly overdrawn: one can accept and enjoy one's needs and welcome them to consciousness if (a) past experience with them has been rewarding, and (b) if present and future gratification can be counted on. For example, if one has in general enjoyed food and if good food is now available, the emergence of appetite into consciousness is welcomed instead of dreaded. ("The trouble with eating is that it kills my appetite.") Something like this is true for thirst, for sleepiness, for sex, for dependency needs and for love needs. However, a far more powerful refutation of the "need-is-a-nuisance" theory is found in the recently merging awareness of, and concern with, growth (self-actualization) motivation.

The multitude of idiosyncratic motives which come under the head of "self-actualization" can hardly be listed since each person has different talents, capacities, potentialities. But some characteristics are general to all of them. And one is that these impulses are desired and welcomed, are enjoyable and pleasant, that the person wants more of them rather than less, and that if they constitute tensions, they are *pleasurable* tensions. The creator ordinarily welcomes his creative impulses, the talented person enjoys using and expanding his talents.

It is simply inaccurate to speak in such instances of tension-reduction, implying thereby the getting rid of an annoying state. For these states are not annoying.

2. Differential Effects of Gratification

Almost always associated with negative attitudes toward the need is the conception that the primary aim of the organism is to get rid of the annoying need and thereby to achieve a cessation of tension, an equilibrium, a homeostasis, a quiescence, a state of rest, a lack of pain.

The drive or need presses toward its own elimination. Its only striving is toward cessation, toward getting rid of itself, toward a state of not wanting. Pushed to its logical extreme, we wind up with Freud's death-instinct.

Angyal, Goldstein, G. Allport, C. Buhler, Schachtel and others have effectively criticized this essentially circular position. If the motivational life consists essentially of a defensive removal of irritating tensions, and if the only end product of tension-reduction is a state of passive waiting for more unwelcome irritations to arise and in their turn, to be dispelled, then how does change, or development or movement or direction come about? Why do people improve? Get wiser? What does zest in living mean?

Charlotte Buhler (22) has pointed out that the theory of homeostasis is different from the theory of rest. The latter theory speaks simply of removing tension which implies that zero tension is best. Homeostasis means coming not to a zero but to an optimum level. This means sometimes reducing tension, sometimes increasing it, e.g., blood pressure may be too low as well as too high.

In either case the lack of constant direction through a lifespan is obvious. In both cases, growth of the personality, increases in wisdom, self-actualization, strengthening of the character, and the planning of one's life are not and cannot be accounted for. Some long-time vector, or directional tendency, must be invoked to make any sense of development through the lifetime (72).

This theory must be put down as an inadequate description even of deficiency motivation. What is lacking here is awareness of the dynamic principle which ties together and interrelates all these separate motivational episodes. The different basic needs are related to each other in a hierarchical order such that gratification of one need and its consequent removal from the center of the stage brings about not a state of rest or Stoic apathy, but rather the emergence into consciousness of another "higher" need; wanting and desiring continues but at a "higher" level. Thus the coming-to-rest theory isn't adequate even for deficiency motivation.

However, when we examine people who are predominantly growth-motivated, the coming-to-rest conception of motivation becomes completely useless. In such people gratification breeds increased rather than decreased motivation, heightened rather than lessened excitement. The appetites become intensified and heightened. They grow upon themselves and instead of wanting less and less, such a person wants more and more of, for instance, education. The person rather than coming to rest becomes more active. The appetite for growth is whetted rather than allayed by gratification. Growth is, *in itself*, a rewarding and exciting process, e.g., the fulfilling of yearnings and ambitions, like that of being a good doctor; the acquisition of admired skills, like playing the violin or being a good carpenter; the steady increase of understanding about people or about the universe, or about oneself; the development of creativeness in whatever field, or, most important, simply the ambition to be a good human being.

Wertheimer (172) long ago stressed another aspect of this same differentiation by claiming, in a seeming paradox, that true goal-seeking activity took up less than 10% of his time. Activity can be enjoyed either intrinsically, for its own sake, or else have worth and value only because it is instrumental in bringing about a desired gratification. In the latter case it loses its value and is no longer pleasurable when it is no longer successful or efficient. More frequently, it is simply not *enjoyed at all,* but only the goal is enjoyed. This is similar to that attitude toward life which values it less for its own sake than because one goes to Heaven at the end of it. The observation upon which this generalization is based is that self-actualizing people enjoy life in general and in practically all its aspects, while most other people enjoy only stray moments of triumph, of achievement or of climax or peak experience.

Partly this intrinsic validity of living comes from the pleasurableness inherent in growing and in being grown. But it also comes from the ability of healthy people to transform means-activity into end-experience, so that even instrumental activity is enjoyed as if it were end activity (97). Growth motivation may be long-term in character. Most of a lifetime may be involved in becoming a good psychologist or a good artist. All equilibrium or homeostasis or rest theories deal only with short-term episodes, each of which has nothing to do with each other. Allport particularly has stressed this point. Planfulness and looking into the future, he points out, are of the central stuff or healthy human nature. He agrees (2) that "Deficit motives do, in fact, call for the reduction of tension and restoration of equilibrium. Growth motives, on the other hand, maintain tension in the interest of distant and often unattainable goals. As such they distinguish human from animal becoming, and adult from infant becoming."

3. Clinical Effects of Gratification

Deficit-need gratifications and growth-need gratifications have differential subjective and objective effects upon the personality. If I may phrase what I am groping for here in a generalized way, it is this: satisfying deficiencies avoids illness; growth satisfactions produce positive health. I must grant that this will be difficult to pin down for research purposes at this time. And yet there is a real *clinical* difference between fending off threat or attack and positive triumph and achievement, between protecting, defending and preserving oneself and reaching out for fulfillment, for excitement and for enlargement. I have tried to express this as a contrast between living fully and *preparing* to live fully, between growing up and being grown.

4. Different Kinds of Pleasure

Erich Fromm (50) has made an interesting and important effort to distinguish higher from lower pleasures, as have so many others before him. This is a crucial necessity for breaking through subjective ethical relativity and is a prerequisite for a scientific value theory.

He distinguishes scarcity-pleasure from abundance-pleasure, the "lower" pleasure of satiation of a need from the "higher" pleasure of production, creation and growth of insight. The glut, the relaxation, and the loss of tension that follows deficiency-satiation can at best be called "relief" by contrast with the *Funktions-lust*, the ecstasy, the serenity that one experiences when functioning easily, perfectly and at the peak of one's powers—in overdrive, so to speak (see Chapter 6).

"Relief," depending so strongly on something that disappears, is itself more likely to disappear. It must be less stable, less enduring, less constant than the pleasure accompanying growth, which can go on forever.

5. Attainable (Episodic) and Unattainable Goal States

Deficiency-need gratification tends to be episodic and climactic. The most frequent schema here begins with an instigating, motivating state which sets off motivated behavior designed to achieve a goal-state, which, mounting gradually and steadily in desire and excitement, finally reaches a peak in a moment of success and consummation. From this peak curve of desire, excitement and pleasure fall rapidly to a plateau of quiet tension-release, and lack of motivation.

This schema, though not universally applicable, in any case contrasts very sharply with the situation in growth-motivation, for here, characteristically, there is no climax or consummation, no orgasmic moment, no end-state, even no goal if this be defined climactically. Growth is instead a continued, more or less steady upward or forward development. The more one gets, the more one wants, so that this kind of wanting is endless and can never be attained or satisfied.

It is for this reason that the usual separation between instigation, goal-seeking behavior, the goal object and the accompanying effect breaks down completely. The behaving is itself the goal, and to differentiate the goal of growth from the instigation to growth is impossible. They too are the same.

6. Species-Wide Goals and Idiosyncratic Goals

The deficit-needs are shared by all members of the human species and to some extent by other species as well. Self-actualization is idiosyncratic since every person is different. The deficits, i.e., the species requirements, must ordinarily be fairly well satisfied before real individuality can develop fully.

Just as all trees need sun, water, and foods from the environment, so do all people need safety, love and status from *their* environment. However, in both cases this is just where real development of individuality can begin, for once satiated with these elementary, species-wide necessities, each tree and each person proceeds to develop in his own style, uniquely, using these necessities for his own private purposes. In a very meaningful sense, development then becomes more determined from within rather than from without.

7. Dependence On, and Independence From, the Environment

The needs for safety, belongingness, love relations and for respect can be satisfied only by other people, i.e., only from outside the person. This means considerable dependence on the environment. A person in this dependent position cannot really be said to be governing himself, or in control of his own fate. He *must* be beholden to the sources of supply of needed gratifications. Their wishes, their whims, their rules and laws govern him and must be appeased lest he jeopardize his sources of supply. He *must* be, to an extent, "other-directed," and *must* be sensitive to other people's approval, affection and good will. This is the same as saying that he must adapt and adjust by being flexible and responsive and by changing himself to fit the external situation. *He* is the dependent variable; the environment is the fixed, independent variable.

Because of this, the deficiency-motivated man must be more afraid of the environment, since there is always the possibility that it may fail or disappoint him. We now know that this kind of anxious dependence breeds hostility as well. All of which adds up to a lack of freedom, more or less, depending on the good fortune or bad fortune of the individual.

In contrast, the self-actualizing individual, by definition gratified in his basic needs, is far less dependent, far less beholden, far more autonomous and self-directed. Far from needing other people, growth-motivated people may actually be hampered by them. I have already reported (97) their special liking for privacy, for detachment and for meditativeness (see also Chapter 13).

Such people become far more self-sufficient and self-contained. The determinants which govern them are now primarily inner ones, rather than social or environmental. They are the laws of their own inner nature, their potentialities and capacities, their talents, their latent resources, their creative impulses, their needs to know themselves and to become more and more integrated and unified, more and more aware of what they really are, of what they really want, of what their call or vocation or fate is to be.

Since they depend less on other people, they are less ambivalent about them, less anxious and also less hostile, less needful of their praise and their affection. They arc less anxious for honors, prestige and rewards.

Autonomy or relative independence of environment means also relative independence of adverse external circumstances, such as ill fortune, hard knocks, tragedy, stress, deprivation. As Allport has stressed, the notion of the human being as essentially reactive, the S-R man, we might call him, who is set into motion by external stimuli, becomes completely ridiculous and untenable for self-actualizing people. The sources of *their* actions are more internal than reactive. This *relative* independence of the outside world and its wishes and pressures, does not mean of course, lack of intercourse with it or respect for its "demand-character." It means only that in these contacts, the self-actualizer's wishes and plans are the primary determiners, rather than stresses from the environment. This I have called psychological freedom, contrasting it with geographical freedom.

Allport's expressive contrast (2) between "opportunistic" and "propriate" determination of behavior parallels closely our outer-determined, inner-determined opposition. It reminds us also of the uniform agreement among biological theorists in considering increasing autonomy and independence of environmental stimuli as the defining characteristics of full individuality, of true freedom, of the whole evolutionary process (156).

8. Interested and Disinterested Interpersonal Relations

In essence, the deficit-motivated man is far more dependent upon other people than is the man who is predominantly growth-motivated. He is more "interested," more needful, more attached, more desirous.

This dependency colors and limits interpersonal relations. To see people primarily as need-gratifiers or as sources of supply is an abstractive act. They are seen not as wholes, as complicated, unique individuals, but rather from the point of view of usefulness. What in them is not related to the perceiver's needs is either overlooked altogether, or else bores, irritates, or threatens. This parallels our relations with cows, horses, and sheep, as well as with waiters, taxicab drivers, porters, policemen or others whom we *use*.

Fully disinterested, desireless, objective and holistic perception of another human being becomes possible only when nothing is needed from him, only when *he* is not needed. Idiographic, aesthetic perception of the whole person is far more possible for self-actualizing people (or in moments of self-actualization), and furthermore approval, admiration, and love are based less upon gratitude for usefulness and more upon the objective, intrinsic qualities of the perceived person. He is admired for objectively admirable qualities rather than because he flatters or praises. He is loved because he is love-worthy rather than because he gives out love. This is what will be discussed below as unneeding love, e.g., for Abraham Lincoln.

One characteristic of "interested" and need-gratifying relations to other people is that to a very large extent these need-gratifying persons are interchangeable. Since, for instance, the adolescent girl needs admiration per se, it therefore makes little difference who supplies this admiration; one admiration-supplier is about as good as another. So also for the love-supplier or the safety-supplier.

Disinterested, unrewarded, useless, desireless perception of the other as unique, as independent, as end-in-himself—in other words, as a person rather than as a tool — is the more difficult, the more hungry the perceiver is for deficit satisfaction. A "high-ceiling" interpersonal psychology, i.e., an understanding of the highest possible development of human relationships, cannot base itself on deficit theory of motivation.

9. Ego-Centering and Ego-Transcendence

We are confronted with a difficult paradox when we attempt to describe the complex attitude toward the self or ego of the growth-oriented, self-actualized person. It is just this person, in whom ego-strength is at its height, who most easily forgets or transcends the ego, who can be most problem-centered, most self-forgetful, most spontaneous in his activities, most homonomous, to use Angyal's term (6). In such people, absorption in perceiving, in doing, in enjoying, in creating can be very complete, very integrated and very pure.

This ability to center upon the world rather than to be self-conscious, egocentric and gratification-oriented becomes the more difficult the more need-deficits the person has. The more growth-motivated the person is the more problem-centered can he be, and the more he can leave self-consciousness behind him as he deals with the objective world.

10. Interpersonal Psychotherapy and Intrapersonal Psychology

A major characteristic of people who seek psychotherapy is a former and/or present deficiency of basic-need gratification. Neurosis can be seen as a deficiency-disease. Because this is so, a basic necessity for cure is supplying what has been lacking or making it possible for the patient to do this himself. Since these supplies come from other people, ordinary therapy *must* be interpersonal.

But this fact has been badly over-generalized. It is true that people whose deficiency needs have been gratified and who are primarily growth-motivated are by no means exempt from conflict, unhappiness, anxiety, and confusion. In such moments they too are apt to seek help and may very well turn to interpersonal therapy. And yet it is unwise to forget that frequently the problems and the conflicts of the growth-motivated person are solved by himself by turning inward in a meditative way, i.e., self-searching, rather than seeking for help from someone. Even in principle, many of the tasks of self-actualization are largely intrapersonal, such as the making of plans, the discovery of self, the selection of potentialities to develop, the construction of a life-outlook.

In the theory of personality improvement, a place must be reserved for self-improvement and self-searching, contemplation and meditation. In the later stages of growth the person is essentially alone and can rely only upon himself. This improvement of an already well person, Oswald Schwarz (151) has called psychogogy. If psychotherapy makes sick people not-sick and removes symptoms, then psychogogy takes up where therapy leaves off and tries to make not-sick people healthy. I was interested to notice in Rogers (142) that successful therapy raised the patients' average score in The Willoughby Maturity Scale from the twenty-fifth to the fiftieth percentile. Who shall then lift him to the seventy-fifth percentile? Or the one hundredth? And are we not likely to need new principles and techniques to do this with?

11. Instrumental Learning and Personality Change

So-called learning theory in this country has based itself almost entirely on deficitmotivation with goal objects usually external to the organism, i.e., learning the best way to satisfy a need. For this reason, among others, our psychology of learning is a limited body of knowledge, useful only in small areas of life and of real interest only to other "learning theorists."

This is of little help in solving the problem of growth and self-actualization. Here the techniques of repeatedly acquiring from the outside world satisfactions of motivational deficiencies are much less needed. Associative learning and canalizations give way more to perceptual learning (123), to the increase of insight and understanding, to knowledge of self and to the steady growth of personality, i.e., increased synergy, integration and inner consistency. Change becomes much less an acquisition of habits or associations one by one, and much more a total change of the total person, i.e., a new person rather than the same person with some habits added like new external possessions.

This kind of character-change-learning means changing a very complex, highly integrated, holistic organism, which in turn means that many impacts will make no change at all because more and more such impacts will be rejected as the person becomes more stable and more autonomous.

The most important learning experiences reported to me by my subjects were very frequently single life experiences such as tragedies, deaths, traumata, conversions, and sudden insights, which forced change in the life-outlook of the person and consequently in everything that he did. (Of course the so-called "working through" of the tragedy or of the insight took place over a longer period of time but this, too, was not primarily a matter of associative learning.)

To the extent that growth consists in peeling away inhibitions and constraints and then permitting the person to "be himself," to emit behavior—"radioactively," as it were—rather than to repeat it, to allow his inner nature to express itself, to this extent the behavior of self-actualizers is unlearned, created and released rather than acquired, expressive rather than coping. (97, p. 180).

12. Deficiency-Motivated and Growth-Motivated Perception

What may turn out to be the most important difference of all is the greater closeness of deficit-satisfied people to the realm of Being (163). Psychologists have never yet been able to claim this vague jurisdiction of the philosophers, this area dimly seen but nevertheless having undoubted basis in reality. But it may now become feasible through the study of self-fulfilling individuals to have our eyes opened to all sorts of basic insights, old to the philosophers but new to us.

For instance, I think that our understanding of perception and therefore of the perceived world will be much changed and enlarged if we study carefully the distinction between need-interested and need-disinterested or desire-less perception. Because the latter is so much more concrete and less abstracted and selective, it is possible for such a person to see more easily the intrinsic nature of the percept. Also, he can perceive simultaneously the opposites, the dichotomies, the polarities, the contradictions and the incompatibles (97, p. 232). It is as if less developed people lived in an Aristotelian world in which classes and concepts have sharp boundaries and are mutually exclusive and incompatible, e.g., male-female, selfish-unselfish, adult-child, kind-cruel, good-bad. A is A and everything else is not-A in the Aristotelian logic, and never the twain shall meet. But seen by self-actualizing people is the fact that A and not-

A interpenetrate and are one, that any person is simultaneously good *and* bad, male and female, adult *and* child. One cannot place a whole person on a continuum, only an abstracted aspect of a person.

We may not be aware when *we* perceive in a need-determined way. But we certainly are aware of it when *we* ourselves are perceived in this way, e.g., simply as a money-giver, a food-supplier, a safety-giver, someone to depend on, or as a waiter or other anonymous servant or means-object. When this happens we don't like it at all. We want to be taken for ourselves, as complete and whole individuals. We dislike being perceived as useful objects or as tools. We dislike being "used."

Because self-actualizing people ordinarily do not have to abstract need-gratifying qualities nor see the person as a tool, it is much more possible for them to take a non-valuing, non-judging, non-interfering, non-condemning attitude towards others, a desirelessness, a "choiceless awareness" (85). This permits much clearer and more insightful perception and understanding of what is there. This is the kind of untangled and uninvolved, detached perception that surgeons and therapists are supposed to try for and which self-actualizing people attain *without* trying for.

Especially when the structure of the person or object seen is difficult, subtle, and not obvious is this difference in style of perception most important. Especially then must the perceiver have respect for the nature of the object. Perception must then be gentle, delicate, unintruding, undemanding, able to fit itself passively to the nature of things as water gently soaks into crevices. It must *not* be the need-motivated kind of perception which *shapes* things in a blustering, over-riding, exploiting, purposeful fashion, in the manner of a butcher chopping apart a carcass.

The most efficient way to perceive the intrinsic nature of the world is to be more receptive than active, determined as much as possible by the intrinsic organization of that which is perceived and as little as possible by the nature of the perceiver. This kind of detached, Taoist, passive, non-interfering awareness of all the simultaneously existing aspects of the concrete, has much in common with some descriptions of the aesthetic experience and of the mystic experience. The stress is the same. Do we see the real, concrete world or do we see our own system of rubrics, motives, expectations and abstractions which we have projected onto the real world? Or, to put it very bluntly, do we see or are we blind?

Needing Love and Unneeding Love

The love need as ordinarily studied, for instance by Bowlby (17), Spitz (159), and Levy (91), is a deficit need. It is a hole which has to be filled, an emptiness into which love is poured. If this healing necessity is not available, severe pathology results; if it *is* available at the right time, in the right quantities and with proper style, then pathology is averted. Intermediate states of pathology and health follow upon intermediate states of thwarting or satiation. If the pathology is not too severe and if it is caught early enough, replacement therapy can cure. That is to say the sickness, "love-hunger," can be cured in certain cases by making up the pathological deficiency. Love hunger is a deficiency disease, like salt hunger or the avitaminoses.

The healthy person, not having this deficiency, does not need to receive love except in steady, small, maintenance doses and he may even do without these for periods of time. But if motivation is entirely a matter of satisfying deficits and thus getting rid of needs, then a contradiction appears. Satisfaction of the need should cause it to disappear, which is to say that people who have stood in satisfying love relationships are precisely the people who should be *less* likely to give and to receive love! But clinical study of healthier people, who have been love-need-satiated, show that although they need less to *receive* love, they are more able to *give* love. In this sense, they are *more* loving people.

This finding in itself exposes the limitation of ordinary (deficiency-need-centered) motivation theory and indicates the necessity for "metamotivation theory" (or growth-motivation or self-actualization theory).

I have already described in a preliminary fashion (97) the contrasting dynamics of B-love (love for the Being of another person, unneeding love, unselfish love) and D-love (deficiency-love, love need, selfish love). At this point, I wish only to use these two contrasting groups of people to exemplify and illustrate some of the generalizations made above.

1. B-love is welcomed into consciousness, and is completely enjoyed. Since it is non-possessive, and is admiring rather than needing, it makes no trouble and is practically always pleasure-giving.

2. It can never be sated; it may be enjoyed without end. It usually grows greater rather than disappearing. It is intrinsically enjoyable. It is end rather than means.

3. The B-love experience is often described as being the same as, and having the same effects as the aesthetic experience or the mystic experience. (See Chapters 6 and 7 on "Peak-Experiences." See also Ref. 104.)

4. The therapeutic and psychogogic effects of experiencing B-love are very profound and widespread. Similar are the characterological effects of the relatively pure love of a healthy mother for her baby, or the perfect love of their God that some mystics have described (69, 36).

5. B-love is, beyond the shadow of a doubt, a richer, "higher," more valuable subjective experience than D-love (which all B-lovers have also previously experienced.) This preference is also reported by my other older, more average subjects, many of whom experience both kinds of love simultaneously in varying combinations.

6. D-love *can* be gratified. The concept "gratification" hardly applies at all to admiration-love for another person's admiration-worthiness and love-worthiness.

7. In B-love there is a minimum of anxiety-hostility. For all practical human purposes, it may even be considered to be absent. There *can*, of course, be anxiety-for-the-other. In D-love one must always expect some degree of anxiety-hostility.

8. B-lovers are more independent of each other, more autonomous, less jealous or threatened, less needful, more individual, more disinterested, but also simultaneously more eager to help the other toward self-actualization, more proud of his triumphs, more altruistic, generous and fostering.

9. The truest, most penetrating perception of the other is made possible by B-love. It is as much a cognitive as an emotional-conative reaction, as I have already emphasized (97, p. 257). So impressive is this, and so often validated by other people's later experience, that, far from accepting the common platitude that love makes people blind, I become more and more inclined to think of the *opposite* as true, namely that non-love makes us blind.

10. Finally, I may say that B-love, in a profound but testable sense, creates the partner. It gives him a self-image, it gives him self-acceptance, a feeling of love-worthiness and respect-worthiness, all of which permit him to grow. It is a real question whether the full development of the human being is possible without it.

Defense and Growth

This chapter is an effort to be a little more systematic in the area of growth theory. For once we accept the notion of growth, many questions of detail arise. Just how does growth take place? Why do children grow or not grow? How do they know in which direction to grow? How do they get off in the direction of pathology?

After all, the concepts of self-actualization, growth and self are all high-level abstractions. We need to get closer to actual processes, to raw data, to concrete, living happenings.

These are far goals. Healthily growing infants and children don't live for the sake of far goals or for the distant future; they are too busy enjoying themselves and spontaneously living for the moment. They are *living*, not *preparing* to live. How can they manage, just being, spontaneously, not *trying* to grow, seeking only to enjoy the present activity, nevertheless to move forward step by step? i.e., to grow in a healthy way? to discover their real selves? How can we reconcile the facts of Being with the facts of Becoming? Growth is not in the pure case a goal out ahead, nor is self-actualization, nor is the discovery of Self. In the child, it is not specifically purposed; rather it just happens. He doesn't so much search as find. The laws of deficiency-motivation and of purposeful coping do not hold for growth, for spontaneity, for creativeness.

The danger with a pure Being-psychology is that it may tend to be static, not accounting for the facts of movement, direction and growth. We tend to describe states of Being, of self-actualization as if they were Nirvana states of perfection. Once you're there, you're there, and it seems as if all you could do is to rest content in perfection.

The answer I find satisfactory is a simple one, namely, that growth takes place when the next step forward is subjectively more delightful, more joyous, more intrinsically satisfying than the last; that the only way we can ever know what is right for us is that it feels better subjectively than any alternative. The new experience validates *itself* rather than by any outside criterion. It is self-justifying, self-validating.

We don't do it because it is good for us, or because psychologists approve, or because somebody told us to, or because it will make us live longer, or because it is good for the species, or because it will bring external rewards, or because it is logical. We do it for the same reason that we choose one dessert over another. I have already described this as a basic mechanism for falling in love, or for choosing a friend, i.e., kissing one person gives more delight than kissing the other, being friends with *a* is more satisfying subjectively than being friends with *b*.

In this way, we learn what we are good at, what we really like or dislike, what our tastes and judgments and capacities are. In a word, this is the way in which we discover the Self and answer the ultimate questions Who am I? What am I?

The steps and the choices are taken out of pure spontaneity, from within outward. The healthy infant or child, just Being, as *part* of his Being, is randomly, and spontaneously curious, exploratory, wondering, interested. Even when he is non-purposeful, non-coping, expressive, spontaneous, not motivated by any deficiency of the ordinary sort, he tends to try out his powers, to reach out, to be absorbed, fascinated, interested, to play, to wonder, to manipulate the world. *Exploring, manipulating, experiencing,* being interested, choosing, delighting, *enjoying* can all be seen as attributes of pure Being, and yet lead to Becoming, though in a serendipitous way, fortuitously, unplanned, unanticipated. Spontaneous, creative experience can and does happen without expectations, plans, foresight, purpose, or goal.[1] It is only when the child sates himself, becomes bored, that he is ready to turn to other, perhaps "higher," delights.

Then arise the inevitable questions. What holds him back? What prevents growth? Wherein lies the conflict? What is the alternative to growth forward? Why is it so hard and painful for some to grow forward? Here we must become more fully aware of the fixative and regressive power of ungratified deficiency-needs, of the attractions of safety and security, of the functions of defense and protection against pain, fear, loss, and threat, of the need for courage in order to grow ahead.

Every human being has *both* sets of forces within him. One set clings to safety and defensiveness out of fear, tending to regress backward, hanging on to the past, *afraid* to grow away from the primitive communion with the mother's uterus and breast, *afraid* to take chances, afraid to jeopardize what he already has, *afraid* of independence, freedom and separateness. The other set of forces impels him forward toward wholeness of Self and uniqueness of Self, toward full functioning of all his capacities, toward confidence in the face of the external world at the same time that he can accept his deepest, real, unconscious Self.

I can put all this together in a schema, which though very simple, is also very powerful, both heuristically and theoretically. This basic dilemma or conflict between the defensive forces and the growth trends I conceive to be existential, imbedded in the deepest nature of the human being, now and forever into the future. If it is diagrammed like this:

Safety◄---------------< PERSON >---------------► Growth

then we can very easily classify the various mechanisms of growth in an uncomplicated way as

a. Enhancing the growthward vectors, e.g., making it more attractive and delight producing,

b. Minimizing the fears of growth,

c. Minimizing the safetyward vectors, i.e., making it less attractive,

d. Maximizing the fears of safety, defensiveness, pathology and regression.

We can then add to our basic schema these four sets of valences:

Enhance the dangers   *Enhance the attractions*
Safety◄< PERSON >►Growth
Minimize the attractions   *Minimize the dangers*

Therefore we can consider the process of healthy growth to be a never ending series of free choice situations, confronting each individual at every point throughout his life, in which he must choose between the delights of safety and growth, dependence and independence, regression and progression, immaturity and maturity. Safety has both anxieties and delights; growth has both anxieties and delights. We grow forward when the delights of growth and anxieties of safety are greater than the anxieties of growth and the delights of safety.

So far it sounds like a truism. But it isn't to psychologists who are mostly trying to be objective, public, behavioristic. And it has taken many experiments with animals and much theorizing to convince the students of animal motivation that they must invoke what P. T. Young (185) called a hedonic factor, over and above need-reduction, in order to explain the results so far obtained in free-choice experimentation. For example, saccharin is not need-reducing in any way and yet white rats will choose it over plain water. Its (useless) taste *must* have something to do with it.

Furthermore, observe that subjective delight in the experience is something that we can attribute to *any* organism, e.g., it applies to the infant as well as the adult, to the animal as well as to the human.

The possibility that then opens for us is very enticing for the theorist. Perhaps all these high-level concepts of Self, Growth, Self-realization, and Psychological Health can fall into the same system of explanation with appetite experiments in animals, free choice observations in infant feeding and in occupational choice, and the rich studies of homeostasis (27).

Of course this formulation of growth-through-delight also commits us to the necessary postulation that what tastes good is also, in the growth sense, "better" for us. We rest here on the faith that if free choice is *really* free and if the chooser is not too sick or frightened to choose, he will choose wisely, in a healthy and growth-ward direction, more often than not.

For this postulation there is already much experimental support, but it is mostly at the animal level, and much more detailed research is necessary with free choice in humans. We must know much more than we do about the reasons for bad and unwise choices, at the constitutional level and at the level of psychodynamics.

There is another reason why my systematizing side likes this notion of growth-through-delight. It is that then I find it possible to tie it in nicely with dynamic theory, with *all* the dynamic theories of Freud, Adler, Jung, Schachtel, Horney, Fromm and Rank, as well as The Self theories of Rogers, Buhler, Combs, Angyal, Allport, Goldstein and of the Growth-and-Being school, Dewey, Rasey, Kelley, Moustakas, Wilson, Perls, Lee, Mearns, etc. (An excellent introduction to most of these writers is (118)).

I criticize the classical Freudians for tending (in the extreme instance) to pathologize everything and for not seeing clearly enough the healthward possibilities in the human being, for seeing everything through brown-colored glasses. But the growth school (in the extreme instance) is equally vulnerable, for they tend to see through rose-colored glasses and generally slide over the problems of pathology, of weakness, of *failure* to grow. One is like a theology of evil and sin exclusively; the other is like a theology without any evil at all, and is therefore equally incorrect and unrealistic.

One additional relationship between safety and growth must be specially mentioned. Apparently growth forward customarily takes place in little steps, and each step forward is made possible by the feeling of being safe, of operating out into the unknown from a safe home port, of daring because retreat is possible. We may use as a paradigm the toddler venturing away from his mother's knee into strange surroundings. Characteristically, he first clings to his mother as he explores the room with his eyes. Then he dares a little excursion, continually reassuring himself that the mother-security is intact. These excursions get more and more extensive. In this way, the child can explore a dangerous and unknown world. If suddenly the mother were to disappear, he would be thrown into anxiety, would cease to be interested in exploring the world, would wish only the return of safety, and might even lose his abilities, e.g., instead of daring to walk, he might creep.

I think we may safely generalize this example. Assured safety permits higher needs and impulses to emerge and to grow towards mastery. To endanger safety, means regression backward to the more basic foundation. What this means is that in the choice between giving up safety or giving up growth, safety will ordinarily win out. Safety needs are prepotent over growth needs. This means an expansion of our basic formula. In general, only a child who feels safe dares to grow forward healthily. His safety needs must be gratified. He can't be *pushed* ahead, because the ungratified safety needs will remain forever underground, always calling for satisfaction. The more safety needs are gratified, the less valence they have for the child, the less they will beckon, and lower his courage.

Now, how can we know when the child feels safe enough to dare to choose the new step ahead? Ultimately, the only way in which we can know is by *his* choices, which is to say only *he* can ever really know the right moment when the beckoning forces ahead overbalance the beckoning forces behind, and courage outweighs fear.

Ultimately the person, even the child, must choose for himself. Nobody can choose for him too often, for this itself enfeebles him, cutting his self-trust, and confusing his *ability* to perceive his own internal delight in the experience, his *own* impulses, judgments, and feelings, and to differentiate them from the interiorized standards of others. [2]

If this is all so, if the child himself must finally make the choice by which he grows forward, since only he can know his subjective delight experience, then how can we reconcile this ultimate necessity for trust in the inner individual with the necessity for help from the environment? For he does need help. Without help he will be too frightened to dare. How can we help him to grow? Equally important, how can we endanger his growth?

The opposite of the subjective experience of delight (trusting himself), so far as the child is concerned, is the opinion of other people (love, respect, approval, admiration, reward from others, trusting others rather than himself). Since others are so important and vital for the helpless baby and child, fear of losing them (as providers of safety, food, love, respect, etc.) is a primal, terrifying danger. Therefore, the child, faced with a difficult choice between his own delight experiences and the experience of approval from others, must generally choose approval from others, and then handle his delight by repression or letting it die, or not noticing it or controlling it by will-power. In general, along with this will develop a disapproval of the delight experience, or shame and embarrassment and secretiveness about it, with finally, the inability even to experience it. [3]

The primal choice, the fork in the road, then, is between others' and one's own self. If the only way to maintain the self is to lose others, then the ordinary child will give up the self. This is true for the reason already mentioned, that safety is a most basic and prepotent need for children, more primarily necessary by far than independence and self-actualization. If adults force this choice upon him, of choosing between the loss of one (lower) vital necessity or another (higher) vital necessity, the child must choose safety even at the cost of giving up self and growth.

(In principle there is no need for forcing the child to make such a choice. People just *do* it often, out of their own sicknesses and out of ignorance. We know that it is not necessary because we have examples enough of children who are offered all these goods simultaneously, at no vital cost, who can have safety and love *and* respect too.)

Here we can learn important lessons from the therapy situation, the creative educative situation, creative art education and I believe also creative dance education. Here where the situation is set up variously as permissive, admiring, praising, accepting, safe, gratifying, reassuring, supporting, unthreatening, non-valuing, non-comparing, that is, where the person can feel completely safe and unthreatened, then it becomes possible for him to work out and express all sorts of lesser delights, e.g., hostility, neurotic dependency. Once these are sufficiently catharted, he then tends spontaneously to go to other delights which outsiders perceive to be "higher" or growthward, e.g., love, creativeness, and which he himself will prefer to the previous delights, once he has experienced them both. (It often makes little difference what kind of explicit theory is held by the therapist, teacher, helper, etc. The really good therapist who may espouse a pessimistic Freudian theory, *acts* as if growth were possible. The really good teacher who espouses verbally a completely rosy and optimistic picture of human nature, will *imply* in actual teaching, a complete understanding and respect for regressive and defensive forces. It is also possible to have a wonderfully realistic and comprehensive philosophy and belie it in practice, in therapy, or teaching or parenthood. Only the one who respects fear and defense can teach; only the one who respects health can do therapy.)

Part of the paradox in this situation is that in a very real way, even the "bad" choice is "good for" the neurotic chooser, or at least understandable and even necessary in terms of his own dynamics. We know that tearing away a functional neurotic symptom by force, or by too direct a confrontation or interpretation, or by a stress situation which cracks the person's defenses against too painful an insight, can shatter the person altogether. This involves us in the question of *pace* of growth. And again the good parent, or therapist or educator *practices* as if he understood that gentleness, sweetness, respect for fear, understanding of the naturalness of defensive and regressive forces, are necessary if growth is not to look like an overwhelming danger instead of a delightful prospect. He implies that he understands that growth can emerge only from safety. He *feels* that if a person's defenses are very rigid this is for a good reason and he is willing to be patient and understanding even though knowing the path in which the child "should" go.

Seen from the dynamic point of view, ultimately *all* choices are in fact wise, if only we grant two kinds of wisdom, defensive-wisdom and growth-wisdom. (See Chapter 12 for a discussion of a third kind of "wisdom," i.e., healthy regression.) Defensiveness can be as wise as daring; it depends on the particular person, his particular status and the particular situation in which he has to choose. The choice of safety is wise when it avoids pain that may be more than the person can bear at the moment. If we wish to help him grow (because we know that consistent safety-choices will bring him to catastrophe in the long run, and will cut him off from possibilities that he himself would enjoy if only he could savor them), then all we can do is help him if he asks for help out of suffering, or else simultaneously allow him to feel safe and beckon him onward to *try* the new experience like the mother whose open arms invite the baby to try to walk. We can't *force* him to grow, we can only *coax* him to, make it more possible for him, in the trust that simply experiencing the new experience will make him prefer it. *Only* he can prefer it; no one can prefer it for him. If it is to become part of him, *he* must like it. If he doesn't, we must gracefully concede that it is not for him at this moment.

This means that the sick child must be respected as much as the healthy one, so far as the growth process is concerned. Only when his fears are accepted respectfully, can he dare to be bold. We must understand that the dark forces are as "normal" as the growth forces.

This is a ticklish task, for it implies simultaneously that we know what is best for him (since we *do* beckon him on in a direction we choose), and also that only he knows what is best for himself in the long run. This means that we must *offer* only, and rarely force. We must be quite ready, not only to beckon forward, but to respect retreat to lick wounds, to recover strength, to look over the situation from a safe vantage point, or even to regress to a previous mastery or a "lower" delight, so that courage for growth can be regained.

And this again is where the helper comes in. He is needed, not only for making possible growth forward in the healthy child (by being "available" as the child desires) and getting out of his way at other times, but much more urgently, by the person who is "stuck" in fixation, in rigid defenses, in safety measures which cut off the possibilities of growth. Neurosis is self-perpetuating; so is character structure. We can either wait for life to prove to such a person that his system doesn't work, i.e., by letting him eventually collapse into neurotic suffering, or else by understanding him and helping him to grow by respecting and understanding both his deficiency needs and his growth needs.

This amounts to a revision of Taoistic "let-be," which often hasn't worked because the growing child needs help. It can be formulated as "helpful let-be." It is a *loving* and *respecting* Taoism. It recognizes not only growth and the specific mechanism which makes it move in the right direction, but it also recognizes and respects the fear of growth, the slow pace of growth, the blocks, the pathology, the reasons for not growing. It recognizes the place, the necessity and the helpfulness of the outer environment without yet giving it control. It implements inner growth by knowing its mechanisms and by being willing to help *it* instead of merely being hopeful or passively optimistic about it.

All the foregoing may now be related to the general motivation theory, set forth in my *Motivation and Personality*, particularly the theory of need gratification, which seems to me to be the most important single principle underlying all healthy human development. The single holistic principle that binds together the multiplicity of human motives is the tendency for a new and higher need to emerge as the lower need fulfills itself by being sufficiently gratified. The child who is fortunate enough to grow normally and well gets satiated and *bored* with the delights that he has savored sufficiently, and *eagerly* (without pushing) goes on to higher more complex, delights as they become available to him without danger or threat.

This principle can be seen exemplified not only in the deeper motivational dynamics of the child but also in microcosm in the development of any of his more modest activities, e.g., in learning to read, or skate, or paint, or dance. The child who masters simple words enjoys them intensely but doesn't stay there. In the proper atmosphere he spontaneously shows eagerness to go on to more and more new words, longer words, more complex sentences, etc. If he is forced to stay at the simple level he gets bored and restless with what formerly delighted him. He *wants* to go on, to move, to grow. Only if frustration, failure, disapproval, ridicule come at the next step does he fixate or regress, and we are then faced with the intricacies of pathological dynamics and of neurotic compromises, in which the impulses remain alive but unfulfilled, or even of loss of impulse and of capacity.[4]

What we wind up with then is a subjective device to add to the principle of the hierarchical arrangement of our various needs, a device which guides and directs the individual in the direction of "healthy" growth. The principle holds true at any age. Recovering the ability to perceive one's own delights is the best way of rediscovering the sacrificed self even in adulthood. The process of therapy helps the adult to discover that the childish (repressed) necessity for the approval of others no longer need exist in the childish form and degree, and that the terror of losing these others with the accompanying fear of being weak, helpless and abandoned is no longer realistic and justified as it was for the child. For the adult, others can be and should be less important than for the child.

Our final formula then has the following elements:

1. The healthily spontaneous child, in his spontaneity, from within out, in response to his own inner Being, reaches out to the environment in wonder and interest, and expresses whatever skills he has,

2. To the extent that he is not crippled by fear, to the extent that he feels safe enough to dare.

3. In this process, that which gives him the delight-experience is fortuitously encountered, or is offered to him by helpers.

4. He must be safe and self-accepting enough to be able to choose and prefer these delights, instead of being frightened by them.

5. If he *can* choose these experiences which are validated by the experience of delight, then he can return to the experience, repeat it, savor it to the point of repletion, satiation or boredom.

6. At this point, he shows the tendency to go on to more complex, richer experiences and accomplishments in the same sector (again, if he feels safe enough to dare.)

7. Such experiences not only mean moving on, but have a feedback effect on the Self, in the feeling of certainty ("This I like; that I don't, for *sure*"); of capability, mastery, self-trust, self-esteem.

8. In this never ending series of choices of which life consists, the choice may generally be schematized as between safety (or, more broadly, defensiveness) and growth, and since only that child doesn't need safety who already has it, we may expect the growth choice to be made by the safety-need gratified child. Only he can afford to be bold.

9. In order to be able to choose in accord with his own nature and to develop it, the child must be permitted to retain the subjective experiences of delight and boredom, as *the* criteria of the correct choice for him. Thealternative criterion is making the choice in terms of the wish of another person. The Self is lost when this happens. Also this constitutes restricting the choice to safety

alone, since the child will give up trust in his own delight-criterion out of fear (of losing protection, love, etc.).

10. If the choice is really a free one, and if the child is not crippled, then we may expect him ordinarily to choose progression forward.[5]

11. The evidence indicates that what delights the healthy child, what tastes good for him, is also, more frequently than not,"best" for him in terms of far goals as perceivable by the spectator.

12. In this process the environment (parents, therapists, teachers) is important in various ways, even though the ultimate choice must be made by the child:

a. it can gratify his basic needs for safety, belongingness, love and respect, so that he can feel unthreatened, autonomous, interested and spontaneous and thus dare to choose the unknown;

b. it can help by making the growth choice positively attractive and less dangerous, and by making the regressive choice less attractive and more costly.

13. In this way the psychology of Being and the psychology of Becoming can be reconciled, and the child, simply being himself, can yet move forward and grow.

The Need to Know and the Fear of Knowing

Fear of Knowledge: Evasion of Knowledge: Pains and Dangers of Knowing

From our point of view, Freud's greatest discovery is that *the* great cause of much psychological illness is the fear of knowledge of oneself—of one's emotions, impulses, memories, capacities, potentialities, of one's destiny. We have discovered that fear of knowledge of oneself is very often isomorphic with, and parallel with, fear of the outside world. That is, inner problems and outer problems tend to be deeply similar and to be related to each other. Therefore we speak simply of fear of knowledge in general, without discriminating too sharply fear-of-the-inner from fear-of-the-outer.

In general this kind of fear is defensive, in the sense that it is a protection of our self-esteem, of our love and respect for ourselves. We tend to be afraid of any knowledge that could cause us to despise ourselves or to make us feel inferior, weak, worthless, evil, shameful. We protect ourselves and our ideal image of ourselves by repression and similar defenses, which are essentially techniques by which we avoid becoming conscious of unpleasant or dangerous truths. And in psychotherapy the maneuvers by which we continue avoiding this consciousness of painful truth, the ways in which we fight the efforts of the therapist to help us see the truth, we call "resistance." All the techniques of the therapist are in one way or another truth-revealing, or are ways of strengthening the patient so he can bear the truth. ("To be completely honest with oneself is the very best effort a human being can make." S. Freud.)

But there is another kind of truth we tend to evade. Not only do we hang on to our psychopathology, but also we tend to evade personal growth because this, too, can bring another kind of fear, of awe, of feelings of weakness and inadequacy (31). And so we find another kind of resistance, a denying of our best side, of our talents, of our finest impulses, of our highest potentialities, of our creativeness. In brief, this is the struggle against our own greatness, the fear of *hubris*.

Here we are reminded that our own Adam and Eve myth, with its dangerous Tree of Knowledge that mustn't be touched, is paralleled in many other cultures which also feel that ultimate knowledge is something reserved for the gods. Most religions have had a thread of anti-intellectualism (along with other threads, of course), some trace of preference for faith or belief or piety rather than for knowledge, or the feeling that *some* forms of knowledge were too dangerous to meddle with and had best be forbidden or reserved to a few special people. In most cultures those revolutionaries who defied the gods by seeking out their secrets were punished heavily, like Adam and Eve, Prometheus and Oedipus, and have been remembered as warnings to all others not to try to be godlike.

And, if I may say it in a very condensed way, it is precisely the god-like in ourselves that we are ambivalent about, fascinated by and fearful of, motivated to and defensive against. This is one aspect of the basic human predicament, that we are simultaneously worms and gods. Every one of our great creators, our god-like people, has testified to the element of courage that is needed in the lonely moment of creation, affirming something new (contradictory to the old). This is a kind of daring, a going out in front all alone, a defiance, a challenge. The moment of fright is quite understandable but must nevertheless be overcome if creation is to be possible. Thus to discover in oneself a great talent can certainly bring exhilaration but it also brings a fear of the dangers and responsibilities and duties of being a leader and of being all alone. Responsibility can be seen as a heavy burden and evaded as long as possible. Think of the mixture of feelings of awe, humility, even of fright that have been reported to us, let us say, by people who have been elected President.

A few standard clinical examples can teach us much. First is the fairly common phenomenon encountered in therapy with women (131). Many brilliant women are caught up in the problem of making an unconscious identification between intelligence and masculinity. To probe, to search, to be curious, to affirm, to discover, all these she may feel as defeminizing, especially if her husband in his uncertain masculinity, is threatened thereby. Many cultures and many religions have kept women from knowing and studying, and I feel that one dynamic root of this action is the desire to keep them "feminine" (in a sadomasochistic sense); for instance, women cannot be priests or rabbis (103).

The timid man also may tend to identify probing curiosity as somehow challenging to others, as if somehow, by being intelligent and searching out the truth, he is being assertive and bold and manly in a way that he can't back up, and that such a pose will bring down upon him the wrath of other, older, stronger men. So also may children identify curious probing as a trespass upon the prerogatives of their gods, the all-powerful adults. And of course it is even easier to find the complementary attitude in adults. For often they find the restless curiosity of their children at least a nuisance and sometimes even a threat and a danger, especially when it is about sexual matters. It is still the unusual parent who approves and enjoys curiosity in his children. Something similar can be seen in the exploited, the downtrodden, the weak minority or the slave. He may fear to know too much, to explore freely. This might arouse the wrath of his lords. A defensive attitude of pseudo-stupidity is common in such groups. In any case, the exploiter, or the tyrant, out of the dynamics of the situation, is not likely to encourage curiosity, learning and knowledge in his underlings. People who know too much are likely to rebel. Both the exploited and the exploiter are impelled to regard knowledge as incompatible with being a good, nice, well-adjusted slave. In such a situation, knowledge *is* dangerous, *quite* dangerous. A status of weakness or subordination, or low self-esteem inhibits the need to know. The direct, uninhibited staring gaze is the main technique that an overlord monkey uses to establish dominance (103). The subordinate animal characteristically drops his gaze.

This dynamic can sometimes be seen, unhappily, even in the classroom. The really bright student, the eager questioner, the probing searcher, especially if he is brighter than his teacher, is too often seen as a "wise guy," a threat to discipline, a challenger of his teachers' authority.

That "knowing" can unconsciously mean domination, mastery, control, and perhaps even contempt, can be seen also from the scoptophiliac, who can feel some sense of power over the naked women he peeps at, as if his eyes were an instrument of domination that he could use for raping. In this sense, most men are peeping Toms and stare boldly at women, undressing them with their eyes. The biblical use of the word "knowing" as identical with sexual "knowing" is another use of the metaphor.

At an unconscious level, knowing as an intrusive, penetrating into, as a kind of masculine sexual equivalent can help us to understand the archaic complex of conflicting emotions that may cluster around the child's peeping into secrets, into the unknown, some women's feeling of a contradiction between femininity and boldly knowing, of the underdog's feeling that knowing is a prerogative of the master, of the religious man's fear that knowing trespasses on the jurisdiction of the gods, is dangerous and will be resented. Knowing, like "knowing," can be an act of self-affirmation.

Knowledge for Anxiety-Reduction And for Growth

So far I have been talking about the need to know for its own sake, for the sheer delight and primitive satisfaction of knowledge and understanding *per se.* It makes the person bigger, wiser, richer, stronger, more evolved, more mature. It represents the actualization of a human potentiality, the fulfillment of that human destiny foreshadowed by human possibilities. We then have a parallel to the unobstructed blooming of a flower or to the singing of birds. This is the way in which an apple tree bears apples, without striving or effort, simply as an expression of its own inherent nature.

But we know also that curiosity and exploration are "higher" needs than safety, which is to say that the need to feel safe, secure, unanxious, unafraid is prepotent, stronger over curiosity. Both in monkeys and in human children this can be openly observed. The young child in a strange environment will characteristically hang on to its mother and only then, venture out little by little from her lap to probe into things, to explore and to probe. If she disappears and he becomes frightened, the curiosity disappears until safety is restored. He explores only out of a safe harbor. So also for Harlow's baby monkeys. Anything that frightens sends them fleeing back to the mother-surrogate. Clinging there, he can first observe and *then* venture out. If she is not there, he may simply curl up into a ball and whimper. Harlow's motion pictures show this very clearly.

The adult human being is far more subtle and concealed about his anxieties and fears. If they do not overwhelm him altogether, he is very apt to repress them, to deny even to himself that they exist. Frequently, he does not "know" that he is afraid.

There are many ways of coping with such anxienes and some of these are cognitive. To such a person, the unfamiliar, the vaguely perceived, the mysterious, the hidden, the unexpected are all apt to be threatening. One way of rendering them familiar, predictable, manageable, controllable, i.e., unfrightening, and harmless, is to know them and to understand them. And so knowledge may have not only a growing-forward function, but also an anxiety-reducing function, a protective homeostatic function. The overt behavior may be very similar, but the motivations may be extremely different. And the subjective consequences are then also very different. On the one hand we have the sigh of relief and the feeling of lowered tension, let us say, of the worried householder exploring a mysterious and frightening noise downstairs in the middle of the night with a gun in his hand when he finds that it is nothing. This is quite different from the illumination and exhilaration, even the ecstasy, of a young student looking through a microscope who sees for the first time the minute structure of the kidney, or who suddenly understands the structure of a symphony or the meaning of an intricate poem or political theory. In the latter instances, one feels bigger, smarter, stronger, fuller, more capable, successful, more perceptive. Supposing our sense organs were to become more efficient, our eyes suddenly keener, our ears unstopped. This is how we would feel. This is what can happen in education and in psychotherapy—and *does* happen often enough.

This motivational dialectic can be seen on the largest human canvases, the great philosophies, the religious structures, the political and legal systems, the various sciences, even the culture as a whole. To put it very simply, too simply, they can represent simultaneously the outcome of the need to understand and the need for safety in varying proportions. Sometimes the safety needs can almost entirely bend the cognitive needs to their own anxiety-allaying purposes. The anxiety-free person can be more bold and more courageous and can explore and theorize for the sake of knowledge itself. It is certainly reasonable to assume that the latter is more likely to approach the truth, the real nature of things. A safety-philosophy or religion or science is more apt to be blind than a growth-philosophy, religion or science.

The Avoidance of Knowledge as Avoidance of Responsibility

Anxiety and timidity not only bend curiosity and knowing and understanding to their own ends, *using* them so to speak, as *tools* for allaying anxiety, but also the lack of curiosity can be an active or a passive *expression* of anxiety and fear. (This is not the same as the atrophy of curiosity through disuse.) That is, we can seek knowledge in order to reduce anxiety and we can also avoid knowing in order to reduce anxiety. To use Freudian language, incuriosity, learning difficulties, pseudo-stupidity can be a defense. Knowledge and action are very closely bound together, all agree. I go much further, and am convinced that knowledge and action are frequently synonymous, even identical in the Socratic fashion. Where we know fully and completely, suitable action follows automatically and reflexly. Choices are then made without conflict and with full spontaneity. But see (32).

This we see at a high level in the healthy person who seems to know what is right and wrong, good and bad, and shows this in his easy, full functioning. But we see this at another level altogether in the young child (or in the child hidden in the adult) for whom thinking about an action can be the same as having acted—"the omnipotence of thought," the psychoanalysts call it. That is, if he has had a wish for the death of his father, he may react unconsciously as if he had actually killed him. In fact, one function of adult psychotherapy is to defuse this childish identity so that the person need not feel guilty about childish thoughts as if they had been deeds.

In any case, this close relation between knowing and doing can help us to interpret one cause of the fear of knowing as deeply a fear of doing, a fear of the consequences that flow from knowing, a fear of its dangerous responsibilities. Often it is better not to know, because if you *did* know, then you would *have* to act and stick your neck out. This is a little involved, a little like the man who said, "I'm so glad I don't like oysters. Because if I liked oysters, I'd eat them, and I *hate* the darn things."

It was certainly safer for the Germans living near Dachau not to know what was going on, to be blind and pseudo-stupid. For if they knew, they would either have had to do something about it or else feel guilty about being cowards.

The child, too, can play this same trick, denying, refusing to see what is plain to anyone else: that his father is a contemptible weakling, or that his mother doesn't really love him. This kind of knowledge is a call for action which is impossible. Better not to know.

In any case, we now know enough about anxiety and cognition to reject the extreme position that many philosophers and psychological theorists have held for centuries, that *all* cognitive needs are instigated by anxiety and are *only* efforts to reduce anxiety. For many years, this seemed plausible, but now our animal and child experiments contradict this theory in its pure form, for they all show that, generally, anxiety kills curiosity and exploration, and that they are mutually incompatible, especially when anxiety is extreme. The cognitive needs show themselves most clearly in safe and non-anxious situations.

A recent book summarizes the situation nicely.

"The beautiful thing about a belief system is that it seems to be constructed to serve both masters at once: to understand the world insofar as possible, and to defend against it insofar as necessary. We do not agree with those who hold that people selectively distort their cognitive functioning so that they will see, remember and think only what they want to. Instead, we hold to the view that people will do so only to the extent that they have to and no more. For we are all motivated by the desire which is sometimes strong and sometimes weak, to see reality as it actually is, even if it hurts" (146, p. 400).

Summary

It seems quite clear that the need to know, if we are to understand it well, must be integrated with fear of knowing, with anxiety, with needs for safety and security. We wind up with a dialectical back and forth relationship which is simultaneously a struggle between fear and courage. All those psychological and social factors that increase fear will cut our impulse to know; all factors that permit courage, freedom and boldness will thereby also free our need to know.

Growth and Cognition

Cognition of Being in the Peak-Experiences

The conclusions in this and in the following chapter are an impressionistic, ideal, "composite photograph" or organization of personal interviews with about eighty individuals, and of written responses by 190 college students to the following instructions:

"I would like you to think of the most wonderful experience or experiences of your life; happiest moments, ecstatic moments, moments of rapture, perhaps from being in love, or from listening to music or suddenly "being hit" by a book or a painting, or from some great creative moment. First list these. And then try to tell me how you feel in such acute moments, how you feel differently from the way you feel at other times, how you are at the moment a different person in some ways." (With other subjects the questioning asked rather about the ways in which the world looked different.)

No one subject reported the full syndrome. I have added together all the partial responses to make a "perfect" composite syndrome. In addition, about fifty people wrote me unsolicited letters after reading my previously published papers, giving me personal reports of peak experiences. Finally, I have tapped the immense literatures of mysticism, religion, art, creativeness, love, etc.

Self-actualizing people, those who have come to a high level of maturation, health, and self-fulfillment, have so much to teach us that sometimes they seem almost like a different breed of human beings. But, because it is so new, the exploration of the highest reaches of human nature and of its ultimate possibilities and aspirations is a difficult and tortuous task. It has involved for me the continuous destruction of cherished axioms, the perpetual coping with seeming paradoxes, contradictions and vagueness and the occasional collapse around my ears of long established, firmly believed in and seemingly unassailable laws of psychology. Often these have turned out to be no laws at all but only rules for living in a state of mild and chronic psychopathology and fearfulness, of stunting and crippling and immaturity which we don't notice because most others have this same disease that we have.

Most frequently, as is typical in the history of scientific theorizing, this probing into the unknown first takes the form of a felt dissatisfaction, an uneasiness over what is missing long before any scientific solution becomes available. For instance, one of the first problems presented to me in my studies of self-actualizing people was the vague perception that their motivational life was in some important ways different from all that I had learned. I first described it as being expressive rather than coping, but this wasn't quite right as a total statement. Then I pointed out that it was unmotivated or metamotivated (beyond striving) rather than motivated, but this statement rests so heavily on which theory of motivation you accept, that it made as much trouble as help. In Chapter 3, I have contrasted growth-motivation with deficiency-need motivations, which helps, but isn't definitive enough yet, because it doesn't sufficiently differentiate Becoming from Being. In this chapter, I shall propose a new tack (into a psychology of Being) which should include and generalize the three attempts already made to put into words, somehow, the observed differences between the motivational and cognitive life of fully evolved people and of most others.

This analysis of states of Being (temporary, metamotivated, non-striving, non-self-centered, purposeless, self-validating, end-experiences and states of perfection and of goal attainment) emerged first from a study of the love-relations of self-actualizing people, and then of other people as well, and finally from dipping into the theological, aesthetic, and the philosophical literatures. It was first necessary to differentiate the two types of love (D-love and B-love), which have been described in Chapter 3.

In the state of B-love (for the Being of the other person or object), I have found a particular kind of cognition for which my knowledge of psychology had not prepared me but which I have since seen well described by certain writers on esthetics, religion, and philosophy. This I shall call Cognition of Being, or for short, B-cognition. This is in contrast to cognition organized by the deficiency needs of the individual, which I shall call D-cognition. The B-lover is able to perceive realities in the beloved to which others are blind, i.e., he can be more acutely and penetratingly perceptive.

This chapter is an attempt to generalize in a single description some of these basic cognitive happenings in the B-love experience, the parental experience, the mystic, or oceanic, or nature experience, the aesthetic perception, the creative moment, the therapeutic or intellectual insight, the orgasmic experience, certain forms of athletic fulfillment, etc. These and other moments of highest happiness and fulfillment I shall call the peak-experiences.

This is then a chapter in the "positive psychology," or "orthopsychology," of the future in that it deals with fully functioning and healthy human beings, and not alone with normally sick ones. It is, therefore, not in contradiction to psychology as a "psychopathology of the average"; it transcends it and can in theory incorporate all its findings in a more inclusive and comprehensive structure which includes both the sick and the healthy, both deficiency, Becoming and Being. I call it Being-psychology because it concerns itself with ends rather than with means, i.e., with end-experiences, end-values, end-cognitions, with people as ends. Contemporary psychology has mostly studied not-having rather than having, striving rather than fulfillment, frustration rather than gratification, seeking for joy rather than having attained joy, trying to get there rather than being there. This is implied by the universal acceptance as an axiom of the a priori definition that all behavior is motivated. (See 97, Chapt. 15).

B-Cognition in Peak-Experiences

I shall present one by one now in a condensed summary, the characteristics of the cognition found in the generalized peak-experience, using the term "cognition" in an extremely broad sense.

1. In *B-cognition the experience or the object tends to be seen as a whole, as a complete unit, detached from relations, from possible usefulness, from expediency, and from purpose.* It is seen as if it were all there was in the universe, as if it were all of Being, synonymous with the universe.

This contrasts with D-cognition, which includes most human cognitive experiences. These experiences are partial and incomplete in ways that will be described below.

We are reminded here of the absolute idealism of the 19th century, in which all of the universe was conceived to be a unit. Since this unity could never be encompassed or perceived or cognized by a limited human being, all actual human cognitions were perceived as necessarily *part* of Being, and never conceivably the whole of it.

2. *When there is a B-cognition, the percept is exclusively and fully attended to.* This may be called "total attention"—see also Schachtel (147). What I am trying to describe here is very much akin to fascination or complete absorption. In such attention the figure becomes *all* figure and the ground, in effect, disappears, or at least is not importantly perceived. It is as if the figure were isolated for the time being from all else, as if the world were forgotten, as if the percept had become for the moment the whole of Being.

Since the whole of Being is being perceived, all those laws obtain which would hold if the whole of the cosmos could be encompassed at once.

This kind of perception is in sharp contrast to normal perception. Here the object is attended to simultaneously with attention to all else that is relevant. It is seen imbedded in its relationships with everything else in the world, and as *part* of the world. Normal figure-ground relationships hold, i.e., both the ground and the figure are attended to, although in different ways. Furthermore, in ordinary cognition, the object is seen not so much *per se* but as a member of a class, as an instance in a larger category. This kind of perception I have described as "rubricizing," (97, Chapt. 14) and again would point out that this is not so much a full perception of all aspects of the objects or person being perceived, as it is a kind of taxonomy, a classifying, a ticketing off into one file cabinet or another.

To a far greater degree than we ordinarily realize, cognition involves also placing on a continuum. It involves a kind of automatic comparing or judging or evaluating. It implies higher than, less than, better than, taller than, etc.

B-cognition may be called non-comparing cognition or non-evaluating or non-judging cognition. I mean this in the sense in which Dorothy Lee (88) has described the way in which certain primitive peoples differ from us in their perceptions.

A person can be seen *per se*, in himself and by himself. He can be seen uniquely and idiosyncratically, as if he were the sole member of his class. This is what we mean by perception of the unique individual, and this is, of course, what all clinicians try to achieve. But it is a very difficult task, far more difficult than we are ordinarily willing to admit. However, it *can* happen, if only transiently, and it *does* happen characteristically in the peak-experience. The healthy mother, perceiving her infant in love, approaches to this kind of perception of the uniqueness of the person. Her baby is not quite like anybody else in the world. It is marvelous, perfect, and fascinating (at least to the extent that she is able to detach herself from Gesell's norms and comparisons with neighbors' children).

Concrete perceiving of the whole of the object implies, also, that it is seen with "care." Contrariwise, "caring" (126) for the object will produce the sustained attention, the repeated examination that is so necessary for perception of all aspects of the object. The caring minuteness with which a mother will gaze upon her infant again and again, or the lover at his beloved, or the connoisseur at his painting will surely produce a more complete perception than the usual casual rubricizing which passes illegitimately for perception. We may expect richness of detail and a many-sided awareness of the object from this kind of absorbed, fascinated, fully attending cognition. This contrasts with the product of casual observation which gives only the bare bones of the experience, an object which is seen in only some of its aspects in a selective way and from a point of view of "importance" and "unimportance." (Is there any "unimportant" part of a painting, a baby, or a beloved?)

3. While it is true that all human perception is a product of the human being and is his creation to an extent, we can yet make some differentiation between the perception of *external objects as relevant to human concerns and as irrelevant to human concerns*. Self-actualizing people are more able to perceive the world as if it were independent not only of them but also of human beings in general. This also tends to be true of the average human being in his highest moments, i.e., in his peak experiences. He can then more readily look upon nature as if it were there in itself and for itself, and not simply as if it were a human playground put there for human purposes. He can more easily refrain from projecting human purposes upon it. In a word, he can see it in its own Being ("endness") rather than as something to be used, or something to be afraid of, or to be reacted to in some other human way.

As one example, let us take the microscope which can reveal through histological slides either a world of *per se* beauty or else a world of threat, danger and pathology. A section of cancer seen through a microscope, if only we can forget that it is a cancer, can be seen as a beautiful and intricate and awe-inspiring organization. A mosquito is a wondrous object if seen as an end-in-itself. Viruses under the electron microscope are fascinating objects (or, at least, they *can* be if we can only forget their human relevance).

B-cognition, because it makes human-irrelevance more possible, enables us thereby to see more truly the nature of the object in itself.

4. One difference between B-cognition and average cognition which is now emerging in my studies, but of which I am as yet uncertain, is that repeated *B-cognizing seems to make the perception richer*. The repeated, fascinated, experiencing of a face that we love or a painting that we admire makes us like it more, and permits us to see more and more of it in various senses. This we may call intra-object richness.

But this so far contrasts rather sharply with the more usual effects of repeated experiencing, i.e., boredom, familiarization effects, loss of attention and the like. I have found to my own satisfaction (although I cannot yet prove it) that repeated exposures to what I consider a good painting will make the painting look *more* beautiful to people preselected as perceptive and sensitive, while repeated exposures to what I consider a bad painting will make it look *less* beautiful. The same is true for women.

In this more usual kind of perception, where so frequently the initial perception is simply a classification into useful or not useful, dangerous or not dangerous, repeated looking makes it become more and more empty. The task of normal perception which is so frequently anxiety-based or D-motivation-determined, is fulfilled in the first viewing. *Need*-to-perceive then disappears, and thereafter the object or person, now that it has been catalogued, is simply no longer perceived. Poverty shows up in repeated experiencing; so, also, does richness. Furthermore, not only does poverty of the percept show up in repeated looking, but also the poverty of the beholder.

One of the main mechanisms by which love produces a profounder perception of the intrinsic qualities of the love object than does non-love is that love involves fascination with the love-object, and therefore repeated and intent and searching looking, seeing with "care." Lovers can see potentialities in each other that other people are blind to. Customarily we say "Love is blind," but we must now make room for the possibility that love may be under certain circumstances more perceptive than non-love. Of course this implies that it is possible in some sense to perceive potentialities which are not yet actual. This is not as difficult a research problem as it sounds. The Rorschach test in the hands of an expert is also a perception of potentialities which are not yet actualized. This is a testable hypothesis in principle.

5. American psychology, or more broadly, Western psychology, in what I consider to be an ethnocentric way, assumes that human needs, fears and interests must always be determinants of perception. The "New Look" in perception is based upon the assumption that cognition must always be motivated. This is also the classical Freudian view (137). The further assumption is implied that cognition is a coping, instrumental mechanism, and that it must to some extent be egocentric. It assumes that the world can be seen *only* from the vantage point of the interests of the perceiver and that the experience must be organized around the ego as a centering and determining point.

I consider this point of view ethnocentric not only because it arises so clearly as an unconscious expression of the Western world outlook, but also because it involves a persistent and assiduous neglect of the writings of philosophers, theologians and psychologists of the Eastern world, particularly of the Chinese, Japanese, and Hindus, not to mention writers like Goldstein, Murphy, C. Buhler, Huxley, Sorokin, Angyal and many others.

My findings indicate that in the normal perceptions of self-actualizing people and in the more occasional peak experiences of average people, *perception can be relatively ego-transcending, self-forgetful, egoless*. It can be unmotivated, impersonal, desireless, unselfish, not *needing*, detached. It can be object-centered rather than ego-centered. That is to say, that the perceptual experience can be organized around the object as a centering point rather than being based upon the ego. It is as if they were perceiving something that had independent reality of its own, and was not dependent upon the beholder. It is possible in the aesthetic experience or the love experience to become so absorbed and "poured into" the object that the self, in a very real sense, disappears. Some writers on aesthetics, mysticism, on motherhood and on love, e.g., Sorokin, have gone so far as to say that in the peak experience we may even speak of identification of the perceiver and the perceived, a fusion of what was two into a new and larger whole, a super-ordinate unit. This could remind us of some of the definitions of empathy and of identification, and, of course, opens up the possibilities of research in this direction.

6. *The peak-experience is felt as a self-validating, self-justifying moment which carries its own intrinsic value with it.* That is to say it is an end in itself, what we may call an end-experience rather than a means-experience. It is felt to be so valuable an experience, so great a revelation, that even to attempt to justify it takes away from its dignity and worth. This is universally attested to by my subjects as they report their love experiences, their mystic experiences, their aesthetic experiences, their creative experiences, and their bursts of insight. Particularly with the moment of insight in the therapeutic situation does this become obvious. By virtue of the very fact that the person defends himself against the insight, it is therefore by definition painful to accept. Its breaking through into consciousness is sometimes crushing to the person. And yet, in spite of this fact, it is universally reported to be worth while, desirable and wanted in the long run. Seeing is better than being blind (172), even when seeing hurts. It is a case in which the intrinsic self-justifying, self-validating worth of the experience makes the pain worthwhile. Numerous writers on aesthetics, religion, creativeness and love uniformly describe these experiences not only as valuable intrinsically, but also as *so* valuable that they make life worth while by their occasional occurrence. The mystics have always affirmed this great value of the great mystic experience which may come only two or three times in a lifetime.

The contrast is very sharp with the ordinary experiences of life, especially in the West, and, most especially, for American psychologists. Behavior is so identified with means to ends that by many writers the words "behavior" and "instrumental behavior" are taken as synonymous. Everything is done for the sake of some further goal, *in order to* achieve something else. The apotheosis of this attitude is reached by John Dewey in his theory of value (38 a), in which he finds no ends at all but only means to ends. Even this statement is not quite accurate because it implies the existence of ends. Rather to be quite accurate he implies that means are means to other means, which in turn are means, and so on ad infinitum.

The peak-experiences of pure delight are for my subjects among the ultimate goals of living and the ultimate validations and justifications for it. That the psychologist should by-pass them or even be officially unaware of their existence, or what is even worse, in the objectivistic psychologies, deny a priori the possibility of their existence as objects for scientific study, is incomprehensible.

7. In *all the common peak-experiences which I have studied, there is a very characteristic disorientation in time and space.* It would be accurate to say that in these moments the person is outside of time and space subjectively. In the creative furor, the poet or artist becomes oblivious of his surroundings, and of the passage of time. It is impossible for him when he wakes up to judge how much time has passed. Frequently he has to shake his head as if emerging from a daze to rediscover where he is. But more than this is the frequent report, especially by lovers, of the complete loss of extension in time. Not only does time pass in their ecstasies with a frightening rapidity so that a day may pass as if it were a minute but also a minute so intensely lived may feel like a day or a year. It is as if they had, in a way, some place in another world in which time simultaneously stood still and moved with great rapidity. For our ordinary categories, this is of course a paradox and a contradiction. And yet this is what is reported and it is therefore a fact that we must take account of. I see no reason why this kind of experiencing of time should not be amenable to experimental research. The judgment of the passing of time in peak-experience must be very inaccurate. So, also, must consciousness of surroundings be much less accurate than in normal living.

8. The implications of my findings for a psychology of values are very puzzling and yet so uniform that it is necessary not only to report them but also to try somehow to understand them. To start at the end first, *the peak-experience is only good and desirable, and is never experienced as evil or undesirable.* The experience is intrinsically valid; the experience is perfect, complete and needs nothing else. It is sufficient to itself. It is felt as being intrinsically necessary and inevitable. It is just as good as it *should* be. It is reacted to with awe, wonder, amazement, humility and even reverence, exaltation and piety. The word sacred is occasionally used to describe the person's reaction to it. It is delightful and "amusing" in a Being sense.

The philosophical implications here are tremendous. If, for the sake of argument, we accept the thesis that in peak-experience the nature of reality itself *may* be seen more clearly and its essence penetrated more profoundly, then this is almost the same as saying what so many philosophers and theologians have affirmed, that the whole of Being is only neutral or good, and that evil or pain or threat is only a partial phenomenon, a product of not seeing the world whole and unified, and of seeing it from a self-centered point of view.

Another way of saying this is to compare it with one aspect of the concept of "god" which is contained in many religions. The gods who can contemplate and encompass the whole of Being and who therefore understand it, must see it as good, just, inevitable, and must see "evil" as a product of limited or selfish vision and understanding. If we could be godlike in this sense then we, too, out of universal understanding would never blame or condemn or be disappointed or shocked. Our only possible emotions would be pity, charity, kindliness and perhaps sadness or B-amusement with the shortcomings of the other. But this is precisely the way in which self-actualizing people do at times react to the world, and in which *all* of us react in our peak moments. This is precisely the way in which all psychotherapists *try* to react to their patients. We must grant, of course, that this godlike, universally tolerant, B-amused and B-accepting attitude is extremely difficult to attain, probably even impossible in a pure form, and yet we know that this is a relative matter. We can approximate it more closely or less closely and it would be foolish to deny the phenomenon simply because it comes rarely, temporarily, and impurely. Though we can never be gods in this sense, we can be more godlike or less godlike, more often or less often.

In any case, the contrast with our ordinary cognitions and reactions is very sharp. Ordinarily we proceed under the aegis of means-values, i.e., of usefulness, desirability, badness or goodness, of suitability for purpose. We evaluate, control, judge, condemn or approve. We laugh-at rather than laugh-with. We react to the experience in personal terms and perceive the world in reference to ourselves and our ends, thereby making the world no more than means to our ends. This is the opposite of being detached from the world, which means in turn that we are not really perceiving it, but perceiving ourselves in it or it in ourselves. We perceive then in a deficiency-motivated way and can therefore perceive only D-values. This is different from perceiving the whole world, or that portion of it which in the peak experience we take as surrogate for the world. Then and only then can we perceive its values rather than our own. These I call the values of Being, or for short, the B-values. These are the same as Robert Hartman's "intrinsic values"(59).

These B-values, so far as I can make out at this point, are—

(1) wholeness; (unity; integration; tendency to one-ness; interconnectedness; simplicity; organization; structure; dichotomy-transcendence; order);

(2) perfection; (necessity; just-right-ness; just-so-ness; inevitability; suitability; justice; completeness; "oughtness");

(3) completion; (ending; finality; justice; "it's finished"; fulfillment; *finis* and *telos*; destiny; fate);

(4) justice; (fairness; orderliness; lawfulness; "oughtness");

(5) aliveness; (process; non-deadness; spontaneity; self-regulation; full-functioning);

(6) richness; (differentiation, complexity; intricacy);

(7) simplicity; (honesty; nakedness; essentiality; abstract, essential, skeletal structure);

(8) beauty; (rightness; form; aliveness; simplicity; richness; wholeness; perfection; completion; uniqueness; honesty);

(9) goodness; (rightness; desirability; oughtness; justice; benevolence; honesty);

(10) uniqueness; (idiosyncrasy; individuality; non-comparability; novelty);

(11) effortlessness; (ease; lack of strain, striving or difficulty; grace; perfect, beautiful functioning);

(12) playfulness; (fun; joy; amusement; gaiety; humor; exuberance; effortlessness);

(13) truth; honesty; reality; (nakedness; simplicity; richness; oughtness; beauty; pure, clean and unadulterated; completeness; essentiality).

(14) self-sufficiency; (autonomy; independence; not-needing-other-than-itself-in-order-to-be-itself; self-determining; environment-transcendence; separateness; living by its own laws).

These are obviously *not* mutually exclusive. They are not separate or distinct, but overlap or fuse with each other. Ultimately they are all *facets* of Being rather than *parts* of it. Various of these aspects will come to the foreground of cognition depending on the operation which has revealed it, e.g., perceiving the beautiful person or the beautiful painting, experiencing perfect sex and/or perfect love, insight, creativeness, parturition, etc.

Not only is this, then, a demonstration of fusion and unity of the old trinity of the true, the good, the beautiful, etc., but it is also much more than that. I have elsewhere reported my finding (97) that truth, goodness and beauty are in the average person in our culture only fairly well correlated with each other, and in the neurotic person even less so. It is only in the evolved and mature human being, in the self-actualizing, fully functioning person that they are so highly correlated that for all practical purposes they may be said to fuse into a unity. I would now add that this is also true for other people in their peak experiences.

This finding, if it turns out to be correct, is in direct and flat contradiction to one of the basic axioms that guides all scientific thought, namely, that the more objective and impersonal perception becomes, the more detached it becomes from value. Fact and value have almost always (by intellectuals) been considered to be antonyms and mutually exclusive. But perhaps the opposite is true, for when we examine the most ego-detached, objective, motivationless, passive cognition, we find that it claims to perceive values directly, that values cannot be shorn away from reality and that the most profound perceptions of "facts" causes the "is" and the "ought" to fuse. In these moments reality is tinged with wonder, admiration, awe and approval i.e., with value.[6]

9. Normal experience is imbedded in history and in culture as well as in the shifting and relative needs of man. It is organized in time and in space. It is part of larger wholes and therefore is relative to these larger wholes and frames of reference. Since it is felt to depend upon man for whatever reality it has, then if man were to disappear, *it* also would disappear. Its organizing frames of reference shift from the interests of the person to the demands of the situation, from the immediate in time to the past and the future and from the here to the there. In these senses experience and behavior are relative.

Peak experiences are from this point of view more absolute and less relative. Not only are they timeless and spaceless in the senses which I have indicated above, not only are they detached from the ground and perceived more in themselves, not only are they relatively unmotivated and detached from the interests of man, but they are also perceived and reacted to as if they were in themselves, "out there," as if they were perceptions of a reality independent of man and persisting beyond his life. It is certainly difficult and also dangerous scientifically to speak of relative and absolute, and I am aware that this is a semantic swamp. And yet I am compelled by the many introspective reports of my subjects to report this differentiation as a finding with which we psychologists will ultimately have to make our peace. These are the words that the subjects themselves use in trying to describe experiences which are essentially ineffable. *They* speak of "absolute," *they* speak of "relative."

Again and again we ourselves are tempted to this kind of vocabulary, for instance, in the realm of art. A Chinese vase may be perfect in itself, may be simultaneously 2000 years old and yet fresh in this moment, universal rather than Chinese. In these senses at least it is absolute, even though also simultaneously relative to time, to the culture of its origin and to the aesthetic standards of the beholder. Is it not meaningful also that the mystic experience has been described in almost identical words by people in every religion, every era, and in every culture. No wonder Aldous Huxley (68a) has called it "The Perennial Philosophy." The great creators, let us say as anthologized by Brewster Ghiselin (54a), have described their creative moments in almost identical terms, even though they were variously poets, chemists, sculptors, philosophers, and mathematicians.

The concept of absolute has made difficulty partly because it has almost always been permeated with a static taint. It is now clear from the experience of my subjects that this is not necessary or inevitable. Perception of an aesthetic object or a beloved face or a beautiful theory is a fluctuating, shifting process but this fluctuation of attention is strictly *within* the perception. Its richness can be infinite and the continued gaze can go from one aspect of the perfection to another, now concentrating on one aspect of it, now on another. A fine painting has many organizations, not just one, so that the aesthetic experience can be a continuous though fluctuating delight as it is seen, in itself, now in one way, now in another. Also it can be seen relatively in one moment, absolutely in the next. We needn't struggle over whether it is *either* relative *or* absolute. It can be both.

10. Ordinary cognition is a very active process. It is characteristically a kind of shaping and selection by the beholder. He chooses what to perceive and what not to perceive, he relates it to his needs and fears and interests, he gives it organization, arranging and rearranging it. In a word, he works at it. Cognition is an energy-consuming process. It involves alertness, vigilance and tension and is, therefore, fatiguing.

B-cognition is much more passive and receptive than active although, of course, it never can be completely so. The best descriptions that I have found of this "passive" kind of cognizing comes from Eastern philosophers, especially from Lao-Tse and the Taoistic philosophers. Krishnamurti (85) has an excellent phrase to describe my data. He calls it "choiceless awareness." We could also name it "desireless awareness." The Taoistic conception of "let be" also says what I am trying to say, namely, that perception may be undemanding rather than demanding, contemplative rather than forceful. It can be humble before the experience, non-interfering, receiving rather than taking, it can let the percept be itself. I am reminded here, also, of Freud's description of "free floating attention." This, too, is passive rather than active, selfless rather than egocentric, dreamy rather than vigilant, patient rather than impatient. It is gazing rather than looking, surrendering and submitting to the experience

I have also found useful a recent memorandum by John Shlien (155) on the difference between passive listening and active forceful listening. The good therapist must be able to listen in the receiving rather than the taking sense in order to be able to hear what is actually said rather than what he expects to hear or demands to hear. He must not impose himself but rather let the words flow in upon him. Only so can their own shape and pattern be assimilated. Otherwise one hears only one's own theories and expectations.

As a matter of fact we may say that it is this criterion, of being able to be receiving and passive, that marks off the good therapist from the poor one of whatever school. The good therapist is able to perceive each person in his own right freshly and without the urge to taxonomize, to rubricize, to classify and pigeon hole. The poor therapist through a hundred years of clinical experience may find only repeated corroborations of the theories which he learned at the beginning of his career. It is in this sense that it has been pointed out that a therapist can repeat the same mistakes for 40 years and then call it "rich clinical experience."

An entirely different, though equally unfashionable, way of communicating the feeling of this characteristic of B-cognition, is to call it, with D. H. Lawrence and other Romantics, non-voluntary rather than volitional. Ordinary cognition is highly volitional and therefore demanding, prearranged, and preconceived. In the cognition of the peak-experience, the will does not interfere. It is held in abeyance. It receives and doesn't demand. We cannot command the peak-experience. It happens *to* us.

11. *The emotional reaction in the peak experience has a special flavor of wonder, of awe, of reverence, of humility and surrender before the experience as before something great.* This sometimes has a touch of fear (although pleasant fear) of being overwhelmed. My subjects report this in such phrases as "This is too much for me." "It is more than I can bear." " It is too wonderful." The experience may have a certain poignancy and piercing quality which may bring either tears or laughter or both, and which may be paradoxically akin to pain, although this is a desirable pain which is often described as "sweet." This may go so far as to involve thoughts of death in a peculiar way. Not only my subjects but many writers on the various peak experiences have made the parallel with the

experience of dying, that is, an eager dying. A typical phrase might be: "This is too wonderful. I don't know how I can bear it. I could die now and it would be all right." Perhaps this is in part a hanging on to the experience and a reluctance to go down from this peak into the valley of ordinary existence. Perhaps it is in part, also, an aspect of the profound sense of humility, smallness, unworthiness before the enormity of the experience.

12. Another paradox with which we must deal, difficult though it is, is found in the conflicting reports of perception of the world. In *some reports, particularly of the mystic experience or the religious experience or philosophical experience, the whole of the world is seen as a unity, as a single rich live entity. In other of the peak experiences, most particularly the love experience and the aesthetic experience, one small part of the world is perceived as if it were for the moment all of the world.* In both cases the perception is of unity. Probably the fact that the B-cognition of a painting or a person or a theory retains all the attributes of the whole of Being, i.e., the B-values, derives from this fact of perceiving it as if it were all that existed at the moment.

13. There are substantial differences (56) between the cognition that abstracts and categorizes and the fresh cognition of the concrete, the raw and the particular. This is the sense in which I shall use the terms abstract and concrete. They are not very different from Goldstein's terms. Most of our cognitions (attendings, perceivings, rememberings, thinkings and learnings) are abstract rather than concrete. That is, we mostly categorize, schematize, classify and abstract in our cognitive life. We do not so much cognize the nature of the world as it actually is, as we do the organization of our own inner world outlook. Most of experience is filtered through our system of categories, constructs and rubrics, as Schachtel (147) has also pointed out in his classical paper on "Childhood Amnesia and the Problem of Memory." I was led to this differentiation by my studies of self-actualizing people, *finding in them simultaneously the ability to abstract without giving up concreteness and the ability to be concrete without giving up abstractness.* This adds a little to Goldstein's description because I found not only a reduction to the concrete but also what we might call a reduction to the abstract, i.e., a loss of ability to cognize the concrete. Since then I have found this same exceptional ability to perceive the concrete in good artists and clinicians as well, even though not self-actualizing. More recently I find this same ability in ordinary people in their peak moments. They are then more able to grasp the percept in its own concrete, idosyncratic nature.

Since this kind of idiographic perceiving has customarily been described as the core of aesthetic perceiving, as for instance by Northrop (127 a), they have almost been made synonymous. For most philosophers and artists, to perceive a person concretely, in his intrinsic uniqueness is to perceive him aesthetically. I prefer the broader usage and think that I have already demonstrated that this kind of perception of the unique nature of the object is characteristic of *all* peak experiences, not only the aesthetic one.

It is useful to understand the concrete perceiving which takes place in B-cognition as a perception of all aspects and attributes of the object simultaneously or in quick succession. Abstracting is in essence a selection out of certain aspects only of the object, those which are of use to us, those which threaten us, those with which we are familiar, or those which fit our language categories. Both Whitehead and Bergson have made this sufficiently clear, as have many other philosophers since, e.g., Vivanti. Abstractions, to the extent that they are useful, are also false. In a word, to perceive an object abstractly means *not* to perceive some aspects of it. It clearly implies selection of some attributes, rejection of other attributes, creation or distortion of still others. We make of it what we wish. We create it. We manufacture it. Furthermore, extremely important is the strong tendency in abstracting to relate the aspects of the object to our linguistic system. This makes special troubles because language is a secondary rather than a primary process in the Freudian sense, because it deals with external reality rather than psychic reality, with the conscious rather than the unconscious. It is true that this lack can be corrected to some extent by poetic or rhapsodic language but in the last analysis much of experience is ineffable and can be put into no language at all.

Let us take for example the perception of a painting or of a person. In order to perceive them fully we must fight our tendency to classify, to compare, to evaluate, to need, to use. The moment that we say this man is, e.g., a foreigner, in that moment we have classified him, performed an abstracting act and, to some extent, cut ourselves off from the possibility of seeing him as a unique and whole human being, different from any other one in the whole world. In the moment that we approach the painting on the wall to read the name of the artist, we have cut ourselves off from the possibility of seeing it with complete freshness in its own uniqueness. To a certain extent then, what we call *knowing*, i.e., the placing of an experience in a system of concepts or words or relations, cuts off the possibility of full cognizing. Herbert Read has pointed out that the child has the "innocent eye," the ability to see something as if he were seeing it for the first time (frequently he is seeing it for the first time). He can then stare at it in wonder, examining all aspects of it, taking in all its attributes, since for the child in this situation, no attribute of a strange object is any more important than any other attribute. He does not organize it; he simply stares at it. He savors the qualities of the experience in the way that Cantril (28, 29) and Murphy (122, 124) have described. In the similar situation for the adult, to the extent that we can prevent ourselves from only abstracting, naming, placing, comparing, relating, to that extent will we be able to see more and more aspects of the many-sidedness of the person or of the painting. Particularly I must underline the ability to perceive the ineffable, that which cannot be put into words Trying to force it into words changes it, and makes it something other than it is, something else *like* it, something similar, and yet something different than *it* itself.

It is this ability to perceive the whole and to rise above parts which characterizes cognition in the various peak experiences. Since only thus can one know a person in the fullest sense of the word, it is not surprising that self-actualizing people are so much more astute in their perception of people, in their penetration to the core or essence of another person. This is also why I feel convinced that the ideal therapist, who presumably should be able as a professional necessity, to understand another person in his uniqueness and in his wholeness, without presupposition, ought to be at least a fairly healthy human being. I maintain this even though willing to grant unexplained individual differences in this kind of perceptiveness, and that also therapeutic experience can itself be a kind of training in the cognition of the Being of another human being. This also explains why I feel that a training in aesthetic perceiving and creating could be a very desirable aspect of clinical training.

14. At *the higher levels of human maturation, many dichotomies, polarities, and conflicts are fused, transcended or resolved.* Self-actualizing people are simultaneously selfish and unselfish, Dionysian and Appolonian, individual and social, rational and irrational, fused with others and detached from others, and so on. What I had thought to be straight-line continua, whose extremes were polar to each other and as far apart as possible, turned out to be rather like circles or spirals, in which the polar extremes came together into a fused unity. So also do I find this as a strong tendency in the full cognition of the object. The more we understand the whole of Being, the more we can tolerate the simultaneous existence and perception of inconsistencies, of oppositions and of flat contradictions. These seem to be products of partial cognition, and fade away with cognition of the whole. The neurotic person seen from a godlike vantage point, can then be seen as a wonderful, intricate, even beautiful unity of process. What we normally see as conflict and contradiction and dissociation can then

be perceived as inevitable, necessary, even fated. That is to say if he can be fully understood, then everything falls into its necessary place and he can be aesthetically perceived and appreciated. All his conflicts and splits turn out to have a kind of sense or wisdom. Even the concepts of sickness and of health may fuse and blur when we see the symptom as a pressure toward health, or see the neurosis as the healthiest possible solution at the moment to the problems of the individual.

15. *The person at the peak is godlike not only in senses that I have touched upon already but in certain other ways as well, particularly in the complete, loving, uncondemning, compassionate and perhaps amused acceptance of the world and of the person,* however bad he may look at more normal moments. The theologians have long struggled with the impossible task of reconciling sin and evil and pain in the world with the concept of an all-powerful, all-loving, all-knowing God. A subsidiary difficulty has been presented by the task of reconciling the necessity of rewards and punishments for good and evil with this concept of an all-loving, all-forgiving God. He must somehow both punish and not punish, both forgive and condemn.

I think we can learn something about a naturalistic resolution of this dilemma from the study of self-actualizing people and from the comparison of the two broadly different types of perception discussed so far, i.e., B-perception and D-perception. B-perception is a momentary thing ordinarily. It is a peak, a high spot, an occasional achievement. It looks as if all human beings perceive most of the time in a deficiency way. That is, they compare, they judge, they approve, they relate, they use. This means that it is possible for us to perceive another human being alternately in two different ways, sometimes in his Being, as if he were the whole of the universe for the time being. Much more often, however, we perceive him as a part of the universe and related to the rest of it in many complex ways. When we B-perceive him, *then* we can be all-loving, all-forgiving, all-accepting, all-admiring, all-understanding, B-amused, lovingly-amused. But these are precisely the attributes assigned to most conceptions of a god (except for amusement—strangely lacking in most gods). In such moments we can then be godlike in these attributes. For instance, in the therapeutic situation we can relate ourselves in this loving, understanding, accepting, forgiving way to all sorts of people whom we normally fear and condemn and even hate—murderers, pederasts, rapists, exploiters, cowards.

It is extremely interesting to me that all people behave at times as if they wanted to be B-cognized (see Chapter 9). They resent being classified, categorized, rubricized. Ticketing off a person as a waiter or a policeman or a "dame" instead of as an individual often offends. We all want to be recognized and accepted for what we are in our fulness, richness and complexity. If such an acceptor cannot be found among human beings, then the very strong tendency appears to project and create a godlike figure, sometimes a human one, sometimes supernatural. Another kind of answer to the "problem of evil" is suggested by the way in which our subjects "accept reality" as being-in-itself, in its own right. It is neither *for* man nor is it *against* him. It just is impersonally what it is. An earthquake which kills poses a problem of reconciliation only for the man who needs a personal God who is simultaneously all-loving, humorless, and omnipotent and who created the world. For the men who can perceive and accept it naturalistically, impersonally and as uncreated, it presents no ethical or axiological problem, since it wasn't done "on purpose" to annoy him. He shrugs his shoulders and if evil is defined anthropocentrically, he simply accepts evil as he does the seasons and the storms. It is in principle possible to admire the beauty of the flood or the tiger in the moment before it kills or even to be amused by it. Of course it is much harder to achieve this attitude with human actions which are hurtful to him, but it is occasionally possible, and the more matured the man is, the more possible it is.

16. *Perception in the peak moment tends strongly to be idiographic and non-classificatory.* The percept, whether a person or the world or a tree or work of art, tends to be seen as a unique instance, and as the only member of its class. This is in contrast to our normal nomothetic way of handling the world which rests essentially on generalization and on an Aristotelian division of the world into classes of various sorts, of which the object is an example or sample. The whole concept of classification rests upon general classes. If there were no classes the concepts of resemblance, of equality, of similarity and of difference would become totally useless. One cannot compare two objects which have nothing in common. Furthermore for two objects to have something in common means necessarily abstraction, e.g., such qualities as redness, roundness, heaviness, etc. But if we perceive a person without abstracting, if we insist upon perceiving all his attributes simultaneously and as necessary to each other, then we no longer can classify. Every whole person from this point of view or every painting or every bird or flower becomes the sole member of a class and must therefore be perceived idiographically. This willingness to see all aspects of the object means greater validity of perception (59).

17. *One aspect of the peak-experience is a complete, though momentary, loss of fear, anxiety, inhibition, defense and control, a giving up of renunciation, delay and*

restraint. The fear of disintegration and dissolution, the fear of being overwhelmed by the "instincts," the fear of death and of insanity, the fear of giving in to unbridled pleasure and emotion, all tend to disappear or go into abeyance for the time being. This too implies a greater openness of perception since fear distorts.

It may be thought of as pure gratification, pure expression, pure elation or joy. But since it is "in the world," it represents a kind of fusion of the Freudian "pleasure principle" and "reality principle." It is therefore still another instance of the resolution of ordinarily dichotomous concepts at higher levels of psychological functioning.

We may therefore expect to find a certain "permeability" in people who have such experiences commonly, a closeness and openness to the unconscious, and a relative lack of fear of it.

18. We have seen that in these various peak-experiences, the person tends to become more integrated, more individual, more spontaneous, more expressive, more easy and effortless, more courageous, more powerful, etc.

But these are similar or almost the same as the list of B-values described in previous pages. There seems to be *a kind of dynamic parallelism or isomorphism here between the inner and the outer. This is to say that as the essential Being of the world is perceived by the person, so also does he concurrently come closer to his own Being* (to his own perfection, of being more perfectly himself). This interaction effect seems to be in both directions, for as he comes closer to his own Being or perfection for any reason, this thereby enables him more easily to see the B-values in the world. As he becomes more unified, he tends to be able to see more unity in the world. As he becomes B-playful, so is he more able to see B-play in the world. As he becomes more strong, so is he more able to see strength and power in the world. Each makes the other more possible, just as depression makes the world look less good, and vice versa. He and the world become more like each other as they both move toward perfection (or as they both move toward loss of perfection) (108, 114).

Perhaps this is part of what is meant by the fusion of lovers, the becoming one with the world in the cosmic experience, the feeling of being *part* of the unity one perceives in a great philosophical insight. Also relevant are some (inadequate) data (180) which indicate that some of the qualities which describe the structure of "good" paintings also describe the good human being, the B-values of wholeness, uniqueness, aliveness. This of course is testable.

19. It will be helpful to some readers if I now attempt briefly to put all of this in another frame of reference which is more familiar to many, the psychoanalytic. Secondary processes deal with the real world outside the unconscious. Logic, science, common sense, good adjustment, enculturation, responsibility, planning, rationalism are all secondary process techniques. The primary processes were first discovered in neurotics and psychotics and then in children, and only recently in healthy people. The rules by which the unconscious works can be seen most clearly in dreams. Wishes and fears are the primary movers for the Freudian mechanisms. The well adjusted, responsible, common-sense man who gets along well in the real world must usually do this in part by turning his back on his unconscious and denying and repressing it.

For me, this realization came most keenly when I had to face the fact years ago that my self-actualizing subjects, picked because they were very mature, were at the same time, also childish. I called it "healthy childishness," a "second naivete." It has also been recognized by Kris (84) and the ego-psychologists as "regression in the service of the ego," not only found in healthy people, but finally conceded to be a *sine qua non* of psychological health. Love has also been conceded to be a regression (i.e., the person who can't regress can't love). And, finally, the analysts agree that inspiration or great (primary) creativeness comes partly out of the unconscious, i.e., is a healthy regression, a temporary turning away from the real world.

Now what I have been describing here may be seen as *a fusion of ego, id, super-ego and ego-ideal, of conscious and unconscious, of primary and secondary processes, a synthesizing of pleasure principle with reality principle, a regression without fear in the service of the greatest maturity, a true integration of the person* at all *levels.*

Redefinition of Self-Actualization

In other words, any person in any of the peak experiences takes on temporarily many of the characteristics which I found in self-actualizing individuals. That is, for the time they become self-actualizers. We may think of it as a passing characterological change if we wish, and not just as an emotional-cognitive-expressive state. Not only are these his happiest and most thrilling moments, but they are also moments of greatest maturity, individuation, fulfillment—in a word, his healthiest moments.

This makes it possible for us to redefine self-actualization in such a way as to purge it of its static and typological shortcomings, and to make it less a kind of all-or-none pantheon into which some rare people enter at the age of 60. We may define it as an episode, or a spurt in which the powers of the person come together in a particularly efficient and intensely enjoyable way, and in which he is more integrated and less split, more open for experience, more idiosyncratic, more perfectly expressive or spontaneous, or fully functioning, more creative, more humorous, more ego-transcending, more independent of his lower needs, etc. He becomes in these episodes more truly himself, more perfectly actualizing his potentialities, closer to the core of his Being.

Such states or episodes can, in theory, come at any time in life to any person. What seems to distinguish those individuals I have called self-actualizing people, is that in them these episodes seem to come far more frequently, and intensely and perfectly than in average people. This makes self-actualization a matter of degree and of frequency rather than an all-or-none affair, and thereby makes it more amenable to available research procedures. We need no longer be limited to searching for those rare subjects who may be said to be fulfilling themselves most of the time. In theory at least we may also search *any* life history for episodes of self-actualization, especially those of artists, intellectuals and other especially creative people, of profoundly religious people, and of people experiencing great insights in psychotherapy, or in other important growth experiences.

The Question of External Validity

So far, I have described a subjective experience in a phenomenological fashion. Its relationship to the external world is another matter altogether. Just because the perceiver *believes* that he perceives more truly and more wholly, is no proof that he actually does so. The criteria for judging the validity of this belief ordinarily lie in the objects or persons perceived or in the products created. They are therefore, in principle, simple problems for correlational research.

But in what sense can art be said to be knowledge? The aesthetic perception certainly has its intrinsic self-validation. It is felt as a valuable and wonderful experience. But so also are some illusions and hallucinations. And furthermore you may be aroused to an aesthetic experience by a painting which leaves me untouched. If we are to go at all beyond the private, the problem of external criteria of validity remains, just as it does with all other perceptions.

The same can be said for loving perception, for the mystic experience, for the creative moment and for the flash of insight.

The lover perceives in the beloved what no one else can, and again, there is no question about the intrinsic value of his inner experience and of the many good consequences for him, for his beloved, and for the world. If we take as an example the mother loving her baby, the case is even more obvious. Not only does love perceive potentialities but it also actualizes them. The absence of love certainly stifles potentialities and even kills them. Personal growth demands courage, self-confidence, even daring; and non-love from the parent or the mate produces the opposite, self-doubt, anxiety, feelings of worthlessness and expectations of ridicule, all inhibitors of growth and of self-actualization.

All personological and psychotherapeutic experience is testimonial to this fact that love actualizes and non-love stultifies, whether deserved or not (17).

The complex and circular question then arises here, "To what extent is this phenomenon a self-fulfilling prophecy?" as Merton has called it. A husband's conviction that his wife is beautiful, or a wife's firm belief that her husband is courageous, to some extent *creates* the beauty or the courage. This is not so much a perception of something that already exists as a bringing into existence by belief. Shall we perhaps consider this an example of perception of a potentiality, since *every* person has the possibility of being beautiful and courageous? If so, then this is different from perceiving the real possibility that someone may become a great violinist, which is *not* a universal possibility.

And yet, even beyond all this complexity, the lurking doubts remain to those who hope ultimately to drag all these problems into the domain of public science. Frequently enough, love for another brings illusions, the perceptions of qualities and potentialities that don't exist, that are not therefore truly perceived but created in the mind of the beholder and which then rest on a system of needs, repressions, denials, projections, and rationalizations. If love can be more perceptive than non-love, it can also be blinder. And the research problem remains to nag us, when is which? How can we select those instances in which perception of the real world is more acute? I have already reported my observations at the personological level, that one answer to this question lies in the variable of the psychological health of the perceiver, in or out of the love relationship. The greater the health, the more acute and penetrating the perception of the world, all other things being equal. Since this conclusion was the product of uncontrolled observation, it must be presented only as a hypothesis awaiting controlled research.

In general, similar problems confront us in aesthetic and intellectual bursts of creativeness, and also in the insight experiences. In both instances, the external validation of the experience is not perfectly correlated with phenomenological self-validation. It is possible for the great insight to be mistaken, the great love to disappear. The poem that creates itself in a peak-experience may have to be thrown away later as unsatisfactory. Creation of a product that will stand up feels subjectively the same as the creation of a product that folds up later under cold, objective critical scrutiny. The habitually creative person knows this well, expecting half of his great moments of insight not to work out. All peak-experiences feel like Being-cognition, but not all are truly so. And yet, we dare not neglect the clear hints that, sometimes at least, greater perspicuity and greater efficiency of cognition can be found in healthier people and in healthier moments, i.e., some peak-experiences *are* B-cognitions. I once suggested the principle that if self-actualizing people can and do perceive reality more efficiently, fully and with less motivational contamination than we others do, then we may possibly use them as biological assays. Through *their* greater sensitivity and perception, we may get a better report of what reality is like, than through our own eyes, just as canaries can be used to detect gas in mines before less sensitive creatures can. As a second string to this same bow, we may use ourselves in our most perceptive moments, in our peak-experiences, when, for the moment, *we* are self-actualizing, to give us a report of the nature of reality that is truer than we can ordinarily manage.

It finally seems clear that the cognitive experiences I have been describing cannot be a substitute for the routine skeptical and cautious procedures of science. However fruitful and penetrating these cognitions may be, and granting fully that they may be the best or only way of discovering certain kinds of truth, yet the problems of checking, choosing, rejecting, confirming and (externally) validating remain with us subsequent to the flash of insight. However, it seems silly to put them into an antagonistically exclusive relationship. It must be obvious by now that they need each other and supplement each other, in about the same way as do the frontiersman and the settler.

The Aftereffects of Peak-Experiences

Completely separable from the question of the external validity of cognition in the various peak-experiences, is that of the aftereffects upon the person of these experiences which in still another sense, may be said to validate the experience. I have no controlled research data to present. I have only the unanimous agreement of my subjects that there *were* such effects, my own conviction that there were, and the complete agreement of all the writers on creativeness, love, insight, mystic experience and aesthetic experience. On these grounds I feel justified in making at least the following affirmations or propositions, all of which are testable.

1. Peak-experiences may and do have some therapeutic effects in the strict sense of removing symptoms. I have at least two reports—one from a psychologist, one from an anthropologist—of mystic or oceanic experiences so profound as to remove certain neurotic symptoms forever after. Such

conversion experiences are of course plentifully recorded in human history but so far as I know have never received the attention of psychologists or psychiatrists.

2. They can change the person's view of himself in a healthy direction.

3. They can change his view of other people and his relations to them in many ways.

4. They can change more or less permanently his view of the world, or of aspects or parts of it.

5. They can release him for greater creativity, spontaneity, expressiveness, idiosyncracy.

6. He remembers the experience as a very important and desirable happening and seeks to repeat it.

7. The person is more apt to feel that life in general is worth while, even if it is usually drab, pedestrian, painful or ungratifying, since beauty, excitement, honesty, play, goodness, truth and meaningfulness have been demonstrated to him to exist.

Many other effects could be reported that are *ad hoc* and idiosyncratic, depending on the particular person, and his particular problems which he considers to be solved or seen in a new light as the result of his experience.

I think that these aftereffects can *all* be generalized and a feeling for them communicated if the peak-experience could be likened to a visit to a personally defined Heaven from which the person then returns to earth. Desirable aftereffects of such an experience, some universal and some individual, are then seen to be practically inevitable.[7]

And may I also emphasize that such aftereffects of esthetic experience, creative experience, love experience, mystic experience, insight experience, and other peak-experiences are preconsciously taken for granted and commonly expected by artists and art educators, by creative teachers, by religious and philosophical theorists, by loving husbands, mothers and therapists and by many others.

On the whole, these good aftereffects are easy enough to understand. What is more difficult to explain is the *absence* of discernible aftereffect in so many people.

Peak-Experiences as Acute Identity-Experiences

As we seek for definitions of identity, we must remember that these definitions and concepts are not now existing in some hidden place, waiting patiently for us to find them. Only *partly* do we discover them; partly also we create them. Partly identity is whatever we say it is. Prior to this of course should come our sensitivity and receptivity to the various meanings the word already has. At once we find that various authors use the word for different kinds of data, different operations. And then of course we must find out something of these operations in order to understand just what the author means when *he* uses the word. It means something different for various therapists, for sociologists, for self-psychologists, for child psychologists, etc., even though for all these people there is also some similarity or overlap of meaning. (Perhaps this similarity is what identity "means" today.)

I have another operation to report, on peak-experiences, in which "identity" has various real, sensible and useful meanings. But no claim is made that these are *the* true meanings of identity; only that we have here another angle. Since my feeling is that people in peak-experiences are *most* their identities, closest to their real selves, most idiosyncratic, it would seem that this is an especially important source of clean and uncontaminated data; i.e., invention is reduced to a minimum, and discovery increased to a maximum.

It will be apparent to the reader that all the "separate" characteristics following are not really separate at all, but partake of each other in various ways, e.g., overlapping, saying the same thing in different ways, having the same meaning in a metaphorical sense, etc. The reader interested in the theory of "holistic analysis" (in contrast to atomistic, or reductive, analysis) is referred to (97, Chap. 3). I shall be describing in a holistic way, not by splitting identity apart into quite separate components which are mutually exclusive, but rather by turning it over and over in my hands and gazing at its different facets, or as a connoisseur contemplates a fine painting, seeing it now in this organization (as a whole), now in that. Each "aspect" discussed can be considered a partial explanation of each of the other "aspects."

1. The person in the peak-experiences feels more integrated (unified, whole, all-of-a-piece), than at other times. He also looks (to the observer) more integrated in various ways (described below), e.g., less split or dissociated, less fighting against himself, more at peace with himself, less split between an experiencing-self and an observing-self, more one-pointed, more harmoniously organized, more efficiently organized with all his parts functioning very nicely

with each other, more synergic, with less internal friction, etc.[8] Other aspects of integration and of the conditions upon which it rests are discussed below.

2. As he gets to be more purely and singly himself he is more able to fuse with the world,[9] with what was formerly not-self, e.g., the lovers come closer to forming a unit rather than two people, the I-Thou monism becomes more possible, the creator becomes one with his work being created, the mother feels one with her child, the appreciator *becomes* the music (and it becomes *him*) or the painting, or the dance, the astronomer is "out there" with the stars (rather than a separateness peering across an abyss at another separateness through a telescope-keyhole).

That is, the greatest attainment of identity, autonomy, or selfhood is itself simultaneously a transcending of itself, a going beyond and above selfhood. The person can then become relatively egoless.[10]

3. The person in the peak-experiences usually feels himself to be at the peak of his powers, using all his capacities at the best and fullest. In Rogers (145) nice phrase, he feels "fully-functioning." He feels more intelligent, more perceptive, wittier, stronger, or more graceful than at other times. He is at his best, at concert pitch, at the top of his form. This is not only felt subjectively but can be seen by the observer. He is no longer wasting effort fighting and restraining himself; muscles are no longer fighting muscles. In the normal situation, part of our capacities are used for action, and part are wasted on restraining these same capacities. Now there is no waste; the totality of the capacities can be used for action. He becomes like a river without dams.

4. A slightly different aspect of fully-functioning is effortlessness and ease of functioning when one is at one's best. What takes effort, straining and struggling at other times is now done without any sense of striving, of working or laboring, but "comes of itself." Allied to this often is the feeling of grace and the look of grace that comes with smooth, easy, effortless fully-functioning, when everything "clicks," or "is in the groove," or is "in overdrive."

One sees then the appearance of calm sureness and Tightness, as if they knew exactly what they were doing, and were doing it wholeheartedly, without doubts, equivocations, hesitations or partial withdrawal. There are then no glancing blows at the target or softened blows, only full hits. The great athletes, artists, creators, leaders and executives exhibit this quality of behavior when they are functioning at their best.

(This is less obviously relevant to the concept of identity than what has gone before, but I think it should be included as an epiphenomenal characteristic of "being one's real self" because it is external and public enough to be researchable. Also I believe it is needed for the full understanding of the kind of godlike gaiety (humor, fun, foolishness, silliness, play, laughter) which I think to be one of the highest B-values of identity.)

5. The person in peak-experiences feels himself, more than at other times, to be the responsible, active, creating center of his activities and of his perceptions. He feels more like a prime mover, more self-determined (rather than caused, determined, helpless, dependent, passive, weak, bossed). He feels himself to be his own boss, fully responsible, fully volitional, with more "free will" than at other times, master of his own fate.

He also looks that way to the observer, for instance, becoming more decisive, looking more strong, more single-minded, more apt to scorn or overcome opposition, more grimly sure of himself, more apt to give the impression that it would be useless to try to stop him. It is as if now he had no doubts about his worth or about his ability to do whatever he decided to do. To the observer he looks more trustworthy, more reliable, more dependable, a better bet. It is often possible to spot this great moment— of becoming responsible—in therapy, in growing up, in education, in marriage, etc.

6. He is now most free of blocks, inhibitions, cautions, fears, doubts, controls, reservations, self-criticisms, brakes. These may be the negative aspects of the feeling of worth, of self-acceptance, of self-love-respect. This is both a subjective and an objective phenomenon and could be described further in both ways. Of course this is simply a different "aspect" of the characteristics already listed and those to be listed below.

Probably these happenings are in principle testable, for objectively these are muscles fighting muscles, instead of muscles synergically helping muscles.

7. He is therefore more spontaneous, more expressive, more innocently behaving (guileless, naive, honest, candid, ingenuous, childlike, artless, unguarded, defenseless), more natural (simple, relaxed, unhesitant, plain, sincere, unaffected, primitive in a particular sense, immediate), more uncontrolled and freely flowing outward (automatic, impulsive, reflexlike, "instinctive," unrestrained, unselfconscious, thoughtless, unaware)[11]

8. He is therefore more "creative" in a particular sense (see Chapter 10). His cognition and his behavior, out of greater self-confidence and loss of doubts, can mold itself in a non-interfering, Taoistic way, or in the flexible way that the Gestalt psychologists have described, to the problematic or unproblematic situation in its intrinsic, "out there" terms or demands (rather than in ego-centered or self-conscious terms), in terms set by the per se nature of the task, or the duty (Frankl), or the game. It therefore is more improvised, extemporized, impromptu, more created out of nothing, more unexpected, novel, fresh, not-stale, non-canting, untutored, unhabitual. It is also less prepared, planned,

designed, premeditated, rehearsed, aforethought, to the extent that these words imply prior time and planning of any sort. It is therefore relatively unsought, non-desired, unneeded, purposeless, unstriven for, "unmotivated," or undriven, since it is emergent and newly created and doesn't come out of prior time.

9. All this can be phrased in still another way as the acme of uniqueness, individuality or idiosyncracy. If all people are different from each other in principle, they are *more* purely different in the peak-experiences. If in many respects (their roles), men are interchangeable, then in the peak-experiences, roles drop away and men become least interchangeable. Whatever they are at bottom, whatever the word "unique self" means, they are more that in the peak-experiences.

10. In the peak-experiences, the individual is most here-now (133), most free of the past and of the future in various senses, most "all there" in the experience. For instance, he can now listen better than at other times. Since he is least habitual and least expectant, he can fully listen without contamination by dragging in expectations based on past situations (which can't be identically like the present one), or hopes or apprehensions based on planning for the future (which means taking the present only as means to the future rather than as end in itself.) Since also he is beyond desire, he needn't rubricize in terms of fear, hate or wish. Nor does he have to compare what is here with what is not here in order to evaluate it (88).

11. The person now becomes more a pure psyche and less a thing-of-the-world living under the laws of the world (see Chapter 13). That is, he becomes more determined by intra-psychic laws rather than by the laws of non-psychic reality insofar as they are different. This sounds like a contradiction or a paradox but it is not, and even if it were, would have to be accepted anyway as having a certain kind of meaning. B-cognition of the other is most possible when there is simultaneously a letting-be of the self *and* of the other; respecting-loving myself *and* respecting-loving the other each permit, support, and strengthen each other. I can grasp the non-self best by non-grasping, i.e., by letting it be itself, by letting it go, by permitting it to live by its own laws rather than by mine, just as I become most purely myself when I emancipate myself from the not-me, refusing to let it dominate me, refusing to live by *its* rules, and insisting on living only by the laws and rules intrinsic to me. When this has happened, it turns out that the intra-psychic (me) and the extra-psychic (other) are not so terribly different after all, and *certainly* are not *really* antagonistic. It turns out that both sets of laws are very interesting and enjoyable and can even be integrated and fused.

The easiest paradigm to help the reader to understand this maze of words is the relationship of B-love between two people but any other of the peak-experiences can also be used. Obviously at this level of ideal discourse (what I call the B-realm) the words freedom, independence, grasping, letting go, trust, will, dependence, reality, the other person, separateness, etc., all take on very complex and rich meanings which they don't have in the D-realm of everyday life, of deficiencies, wants, needs, self-preservation and of dichotomies, polarities and splits.

12. There are certain theoretical advantages in stressing now the aspect of non-striving or non-needing and taking it as the centering-point (or center of organization) of the something we are studying. In various ways described above, and with certain delimited meanings, the person in the peak-experience becomes unmotivated (or un-driven), especially from the point of view of the deficiency needs. In this same realm of discourse, it makes similar sense to describe highest, most authentic identity as non-striving, non-needing, non-wishing, i.e., as having transcended needs and drives of the ordinary sort. He just is. Joy has been attained which means a temporary end to the *striving* for joy.

Something of the sort has already been described for the self-actualizing person. Everything now comes of its own accord, pouring out, without will, effortlessly, purposelessly. He acts now totally and without deficiency, not homeostatically or need-reductively, not to avoid pain or displeasure or death, not for the sake of a goal further on in the future, not for any other end than itself. His behavior and experience becomes *per se*, and self-validating, end-behavior and end-experience, rather than means-behavior or means-experience.

At this level, I have called the person godlike because most gods have been considered to have no needs or wants, no deficiencies, nothing lacking, to be gratified in all things. The characteristics and especially the actions of the "highest," "best" gods have then been deduced as based upon not-wanting. I have found these deductions very stimulating in trying to understand the actions of human beings when *they* act from non-wanting. For instance, I find this a very illuminating base for the theory of godlike humor and amusement, the theory of boredom, the theory of creativeness, etc. The fact that the human embryo also has no needs is a fertile source of confusion between the high Nirvana and the low Nirvana discussed in Chapter 11.

13. Expression and communication in the peak-experiences tend often to become poetic, mythical and rhapsodic, as if this were the natural kind of language to express such states of being. I have only recently become aware of

this in my subjects and in myself so shouldn't say much about it. Chapter 15 is also relevant. The implication for identity theory is that more authentic persons may, by that very fact, become more like poets, artists, musicians, prophets, etc.[12]

14. All peak-experiences may be fruitfully understood as completions-of-the-act in David M. Levy's sense (90), or as the Gestalt psychologists' closure, or on the paradigm of the Reichian type of complete orgasm, or as total discharge, catharsis, culmination, climax, consummation, emptying or finishing (106). Contrast is with the perseveration of incompleted problems, with the partially emptied breast or prostate gland, with the incomplete bowel movement, with not being able to weep away grief, with the partial satiation of hunger in the dieter, with the kitchen that never gets fully clean, with coitus reservatus, with the anger which must remain unexpressed, with the athlete who has had no exercise, with not being able to straighten the crooked picture on the wall, with having to swallow stupidity, inefficiency or injustice, etc. From these examples, any reader should be able to understand phenomenologically how important completion is, and also why this viewpoint is so helpful in enriching the understanding of non-striving, integration, relaxation and everything else that has gone before. Completion seen out in the world is perfection, justice, beauty, end rather than means, etc. (106). Since the outer and inner world are to some extent isomorphic and are dialectically related ("cause" each other), we come to the edge of the problem of how the good person and the good world make each other.

How does this bear on identity? Probably the authentic person is himself complete or final in some sense; he certainly experiences subjective finality, completion or perfection at times; and he certainly perceives it in the world. It *may* turn out that *only* peakers can achieve full identity; that non-peakers must always remain incomplete, deficient, striving, lacking something, living among means rather than among ends; or if the correlation turns out not to be perfect, I am certain at least that it is positive, between authenticity and peak-experiencing.

As we consider the physical and psychological tensions and perseverations of incompleteness, it seems plausible that they may be incompatible not only with serenity, peacefulness and psychological well-being, but also with physical well-being. We may also have a clue here to the puzzling finding that many people report their peak-experiences as if they were somehow akin to (beautiful) death, as if the most poignant living had a paradoxical something of eager or willing dying in it, too. It may be that any perfect completion or end is metaphorically, mythologically or archaically a death, as Rank implies (76, 121).

15. I very strongly feel that playfulness of a certain kind is one of the B-values. Some of the reasons for thinking so have already been touched upon. One of the most important is that it is fairly often reported in the peak-experiences (both within the person and perceived in the world) and also can be perceived by the investigator from outside the person reporting.

It is very hard to describe this B-playfulness since the English language falls far short here (as *in general* it is unable to describe the "higher" subjective experiences). It has a cosmic or a godlike, good-humored quality, certainly transcending hostility of any kind. It could as easily be called happy joy, or gay exuberance or delight. It has a quality of spilling over as of richness or surplus (not D-motivated). It is existential in the sense that it is an amusement or delight with both the smallness (weakness) and the largeness (strength) of the human being, transcending the dominance-subordinance polarity. It has a certain quality of triumph in it, sometimes perhaps also of relief. It is simultaneously mature and childlike.

It is final, Utopian, Eupsychian, transcendent in the sense in which Marcuse (93) and Brown (19) have described. It could also be called Nietzschean.

Intrinsically involved with it as part of its definition are ease, effortlessness, grace, good fortune, relief from inhibitions, restraints and doubts, amusement-with (not-at) B-cognition, transcendance of ego-centering and means-centering, transcendance of time and space, of history, of localism.

And finally, it is in itself an integrator, as beauty is, or love, or the creative intellect. This is in the sense that it is a resolver of dichotomies, a solution to many insoluble problems. It is one good solution of the human situation, teaching us that one way of solving a problem is to be amused by it. It enables us to live simultaneously in the D-realm and in the B-realm, to be at the same time Don Quixote and Sancho Panza.

16. People during and after peak-experiences characteristically feel lucky, fortunate, graced. A not uncommon reaction is "I don't deserve this." Peaks are not planned or brought about by design; they happen. We are "surprised by joy" (91 a). The reaction of surprise, of unexpectedness, of the sweet "shock of recognition" are very frequent.

A common consequence is a feeling of gratitude, in religious persons to their God, in others to Fate, to Nature, to people, to the past, to parents, to the world, to everything and anything that helped to make this wonder possible. This can go over into worship, giving thanks, adoring, giving praise, oblation, and other reactions which fit very easily into a religious framework. Clearly any psychology of religion, either supernatural or natural, must take account of these happenings, as also must any naturalistic theory of the origins of religion.

Very often this feeling of gratitude is expressed as or leads to an all-embracing love for everybody and everything, to a perception of the world as beautiful, and good, often to an impulse to do something good for the world, an eagerness to repay, even a sense of obligation.

Finally, it is quite probable that we have here the theoretical link to the described facts of humility and pride in self-actualizing, authentic persons. The lucky person could hardly take full credit for his luck, nor could the awed person, nor the grateful person. He must ask himself the question "Do I deserve this?" Such people resolve the dichotomy between pride and humility by fusing them into a single, complex, superordinate unity, that is, by being proud (in a certain sense) and humble (in a certain sense). Pride (tinctured with humility) is not *hubris* or paranoia; humility (tinctured with pride) is not masochism. Only dichotomizing them pathologizes them. B-gratitude enables us to integrate within one skin the hero and the humble servant.

Concluding Remark

I wish to underscore one main paradox I have dealt with above (number 2) which we must face even if we don't understand it. The goal of identity (self-actualization, autonomy, individuation, Horney's real self, authenticity, etc.) seems to be simultaneously an end-goal in itself, and also a transitional goal, a rite of passage, a step along the path to the transcendence of identity. This is like saying its function is to erase itself. Put the other way about, if our goal is the Eastern one of ego-transcendence and obliteration, of leaving behind self-consciousness and self-observation, of fusion with the world and identification with it (Bucke), of homonomy (Angyal), then it looks as if the best path to this goal for most people is via achieving identity, a strong real self, and via basic-need-gratification rather than via asceticism.

Perhaps it is relevant to this theory that my young subject tend to report *two* kinds of physical reaction to peak-experiences. One is excitement and high tension ("I feel wild, like jumping up and down, like yelling out loud"). The other is relaxation, peacefulness, quietness, the feeling of stillness. For instance, after a beautiful sex experience, or esthetic experience or creative furor, *either* is possible; either continued high excitement, inability to sleep, or lack of wish for it, even loss of appetite, constipation, etc. Or else, complete relaxation, inaction, deep sleep, etc. What this means I don't know.

Some Dangers of Being-Cognition

The aim of this chapter is to correct the widespread misunderstanding of self-actualization as a static, unreal, "perfect" state in which all human problems are transcended, and in which people "live happily forever after" in a superhuman state of serenity or ecstasy. This is empirically not so, as I have previously pointed out (97).

To make this fact clearer, I could describe self-actualization as a development of personality which frees the person from the deficiency problems of youth, and from the neurotic (or infantile, or fantasy, or unnecessary, or "unreal") problems of life, so that he is able to face, endure and grapple with the "real" problems of life (the intrinsically and ultimately human problems, the unavoidable, the "existential" problems to which there is no perfect solution). That is, it is not an absence of problems but a moving from transitional or unreal problems to real problems. For shock purposes, I could even call the self-actualizing person a self-accepting and insightful neurotic, for this phrase may be defined in such a way as to be almost synonymous with "understanding and accepting the intrinsic human situation," i.e., facing and accepting courageously, and even enjoying, being amused by the "shortcomings" of human nature instead of trying to deny them.

It is these real problems which confront even (or especially) the most highly matured human beings, that I would like to deal with in the future, e.g., real guilt, real sadness, real loneliness, healthy selfishness, courage, responsibility, responsibility for others, etc.

Of course there is a quantitative (as well as qualitative) improvement that comes with higher personality evolvement, quite apart from the intrinsic satisfaction of seeing the truth rather than fooling oneself. Most human guilt, statistically speaking, is neurotic rather than real guilt. Being freed of neurotic guilt means absolutely to have lesser amounts of guilt, even though the probability of real guilt remains.

Not only this, but highly evolved personalities also have more peak-experiences, and these seem to be more profound (even though this may be less true of the "obsessional" or Appolonian type of self-actualization). That is to say, though being more fully human means to have problems and pains still (even though of a "higher" sort), yet it remains true that these problems and pains are quantitatively less, and that the pleasures are quantitatively and qualitatively greater. In a word, an individual is subjectively better off for having reached a higher level of personal development.

Self-actualizing people have been found more capable than the average population of a particular kind of cognition which I have called Being-cognition. This has been described in Chapter 6 as cognition of the essence, or "is-ness," or intrinsic structure and dynamics, and presently existing potentialities of something or someone or everything. B-cognition (B = being) is in contrast to D-cognition (D = deficiency-need-motivation) or human-centered and self-centered cognition. Just as self-actualization does not mean absence of problems, so does B-cognition as one aspect of it hold certain dangers.

Dangers of B-Cognition

1. *The main danger of B-cognition is of making action impossible or at least indecisive.* B-cognition is without judgment, comparison, condemnation or evaluation. Also it is without decision, because decision is readiness to act, and B-cognition is passive contemplation, appreciation, and non-interfering, i.e., "let-be." So long as one contemplates the cancer or the bacteria, awe-struck, admiring, wondering, passively drinking in the delight of rich understanding, then one does nothing. Anger, fear, desire to improve the situation, to destroy or kill, condemnation, human-centered conclusions ("This is bad for me," or, "This is my enemy and will hurt me") are all in abeyance. Wrong or right, good or evil, the past and the future, all have nothing to do with B-cognition, and are at the same time inoperative. It is not in-the-world, in the existentialist sense. It is not even human in the ordinary sense either; it is godlike, compassionate, non-active, non-interfering, non-doing. It has nothing to do with friends or enemies in the human-centered sense. It is only when the cognition shifts over to D-cognition that action, decision, judgment, punishment, condemnation, planning for the future becomes possible (88).

The main danger, then, is that B-cognition is at the moment incompatible with action.[13] But since we, most of the time, live in-the-world, *action is necessary* (defensive or offensive action, or selfishly centered action in the terms of the beholder rather than of the beheld). A tiger has a right to live (as do flies, or mosquitoes, or bacteria) from the point of view of its own "being"; but also so does a human being. And *there* is the unavoidable conflict. The demands of self-actualization may necessitate killing the tiger, even though B-cognition of the tiger is against killing the tiger. That is, even existentially, intrinsic and necessary to the concept of self-actualization, is a certain selfishness and self-protectiveness, a certain promise of necessary violence, even of ferocity. And therefore, self-actualization demands not only B-cognition but also D-cognition as a necessary aspect of itself. This means then that conflict and practical decisiveness and choice are necessarily involved in the concept of self-actualization. This means that fighting, struggle, striving, uncertainty, guilt, regret must also be "necessary" epiphenomena of self-actualization. It means that self-actualization involves *both* contemplation and action *necessarily.*

Now it is possible in a society that there be a certain division of labor. Contemplators may be exempted from action, if someone else can do the acting. We don't have to butcher our own beefsteaks. Goldstein (55, 56) has pointed this out in a widely generalized form. Just as his brain-impaired patients can live without abstraction and without catastrophic anxiety because other people protect them and do for them what they themselves cannot do, so does self-actualization in general, at least in so far as it is a specialized kind, become possible because other people permit it and help it. (My colleague, Walter Toman, in conversations, has also stressed that well-rounded self-actualization becomes less and less possible in a specialized society.) Einstein, a highly specialized person in his last years, was made possible by his wife, by Princeton, by friends, etc. Einstein could give up versatility, and self-actualize because other people did for him. On a desert island, alone, he *might* have self-actualized in Goldstein's sense ("doing the best with his capacities that the world permits"), but at any rate it could not have been the specialized self-actualization that it was. And maybe it would have been impossible altogether, i.e., he might have died or become anxious and inferior over his demonstrated incapacities, or he might have slipped back to living at the D-need level.

2. *Another danger of B-cognition and of contemplative understanding is that it may make us less responsible especially in helping other people.* The extreme case is the infant. To "let-be" means to hinder him or even to kill him. We also have responsibility for non-infants, adults, animals, the soil, the trees, the flowers. The surgeon who gets lost in peak-wonder at the beautiful tumor may kill his patient. If we admire the flood, we don't build the dam. And this is true not only for the other people who suffer from the results of non-action, but also for the contemplator himself, since he must surely feel guilty at the bad effects upon others of his contemplation and non-action. (He *must* feel guilty because he "loves" them in one way or another; he is love-identified with his 'brothers,' and this means care for *their* self-actualization, which their death or suffering would cut off.)

The best examples of this dilemma are found in the teacher's attitude toward his students, the parent's attitude toward his children, and the therapist's attitude toward his patients. Here it is easy to see the relationship to be a relationship-of-its-own-kind. But we must also face the necessities that come from the teacher's (parent's, therapist's) responsibility in fostering growth, i.e., the problems of setting limits, of discipline, of punishment, of *not* gratifying, of deliberately being the frustrator, of being able to arouse and endure hostility, etc.

3. *Inhibition of action, and loss of responsibility leads to fatalism*, i.e., "What will be will be. The world is as it is. It is determined. I can do nothing about it." This is a loss of voluntarism, of free will, a bad theory of determinism, and is certainly harmful to everybody's growth and self-actualization.

4. *Inactive contemplation will almost necessarily be misunderstood by others who suffer from it.* They will think it to be lack of love, of concern, of compassion. This will not only stop growth toward self-actualization in them, but may also send them backwards in the growth incline since it can "teach" them that the world is bad, and that people are bad. As a consequence, their love, respect and trust in people will retrogress. This means then worsening the world especially for children and adolescents and weak adults. They interpret "let-be" as neglect, or lack of love, or even contempt.

5. *Pure contemplation involves, as a special case of the above, not writing, not helping, not teaching.* The Buddhists distinguish the Pratyekabuddha, who wins enlightenment only for himself, independently of others, from the Bodhisattva who, having attained enlightenment, yet feels that his own salvation is imperfect so long as others are unenlightened. For the sake of his own self-actualization, we may say, he must turn away from the bliss of B-cognition in order to help others and teach them (25).

Was Buddha's enlightenment a purely personal, private possession? Or did it also necessarily belong to others, to the world? Writing and teaching, it is true, are often (not always) steps back from bliss or ecstasy. It means giving up heaven to help others get there. Is the Zen Buddhist or the Taoist correct, who says, "As soon as you talk about it, it no longer exists, and is no longer true" (i.e., since the *only* way to experience it is to experience it, and anyway words could never describe it, since it is ineffable)?

Of course there is some right on both sides. (That is why it is an existential dilemma, eternal, unsolvable.) If I find an oasis which other people could share, shall I enjoy it myself or save their lives by leading them there? If I find a Yosemite which is beautiful partly because it is quiet and non-human and private, shall I keep it or make it into a National Park for millions of people who, because they are millions, will make it less than it was or even destroy it? Shall I share my private beach with them and make it thereby unprivate? How right is the Indian who respects life and hates active killing and thereby lets the cows get fat while the babies die? What degree of enjoyment of food may I allow myself in a poor country where the starving children look on? Ought I starve too? There is no nice, clean, theoretical, a priori answer. No matter what answer is given, there must be some regret at least. Self-actualization must be selfish; and it must be unselfish. And so there must be choice, conflict, and the possibility of regret.

Maybe the principle of division of labor (tied in with the principle of individual constitutional differences) could help toward a better answer (although never toward a perfect answer). As in various religious orders some feel the call to "selfish self-actualization," and some feel the call to "doing good self-actualization," maybe the society could ask, as a favor (thereby relieving guilt), that some people become "selfish self-actualizers," pure contemplators. The society could assume that it would be worth its while to support such people for the good example they would set others, the inspiration, and the demonstration of the possibility that pure, out-of-the-world contemplation can exist. We do this for a few of our great scientists, artists, writers and philosophers. We relieve them of teaching, writing and social responsibilities not only for "pure" reasons, but also in a gamble that this will pay off for us as well.

This dilemma also complicates the problem of "real guilt" (Fromm's "humanistic guilt") as I have called it, to differentiate it from neurotic guilt. Real guilt comes from not being true to yourself, to your own fate in life, to your own intrinsic nature; see also Mowrer (119) and Lynd (92).

But here we raise the further question, "What kind of guilt comes from being true to yourself but not to others?" As we have seen, being true to yourself may at times intrinsically and necessarily be in conflict with being true to others. A choice is both possible and necessary. And the choice can only rarely be completely satisfactory. If, as Goldstein teaches, you must be true to others in order to be true to yourself (55), and as Adler states, social interest is an intrinsic, defining aspect of mental health (8), then the world must be sorry as the self-actualizing person sacrifices some portion of himself in order to save another person. If, on the other hand, you must *first* be true to yourself, then the world must be sorry over the unwritten manuscripts, the paintings thrown away, the lessons we could have learned, from our pure (and selfish) contemplators who have no thought for helping us.

6. *B-cognition can lead to undiscriminating acceptance, to blurring of everyday values, to loss of taste, to too great tolerance.* This is so because every person, seen from the viewpoint of his own Being exclusively, is seen as perfect in his own kind. Evaluation, condemnation, judging, disapproval, criticism, comparison are all then inapplicable and beside the point (88). While unconditional

acceptance is a *sine qua non* for the therapist, let us say, or for the lover, the teacher, the parent, the friend, it is clearly not alone sufficient for the judge, the policeman, or the administrator.

We already recognize a certain incompatibility in the two interpersonal attitudes implied here. Most psychotherapists will refuse to assume any disciplining or punishing function for their patients. And many executives, administrators, or generals will refuse to take on any therapeutic or personal responsibility for the people to whom they give orders and whom they have to discharge or punish.

The dilemma for almost all people is posed by the necessity for being both "therapist" and "policeman" at various times. And we may expect that the more fully-human person, taking both roles more seriously, will probably be more troubled by this dilemma than is the average person, who is often not even aware that there *is* any dilemma.

Perhaps for this reason, perhaps for others, self-actualizing people so far studied are generally able to combine the two functions well, by being most often compassionate and understanding and yet also more capable of righteous indignation than the average person. Some data are available to indicate that self-actualizing people and healthier college students give vent to their justified indignation and disapproval more wholeheartedly and with less uncertainty than do average people.

Unless the capacity for compassion-through-understanding is supplemented by the capacity for anger, disapproval, and indignation, the result may be a flattening of all affect, a blandness in reaction to people, an inability to be indignant, and a loss of discrimination of and taste for real capacity, skill, superiority, and excellence. This may turn out to be an occupational hazard for professional B-cognizers if we can take at face value the widespread impression that many psychotherapists seem rather too neutral and unreactive, too bland, too even, too unfiery in their social relations.

7. *B-cognition of another person amounts to perceiving him as "perfect" in a certain sense which he can very easily misinterpret.* To be unconditionally accepted, to be loved utterly, to be approved of completely, can be, as we know, wonderfully strengthening and growth-promoting, highly therapeutic and psychogogic. And yet, we must now be aware, this attitude can also be misperceived as an intolerable demand to live up to unreal and perfectionistic expectations. The more unworthy and imperfect he feels, and the more he misinterprets the words "perfect" and "acceptance," the more he will feel this attitude to be a burden.

Actually, of course, the word "perfect" has two meanings, one for the realm of Being, the other for the realm of Deficiency, of striving, and of becoming. In B-cognition, "perfection" means totally realistic perceiving *and* acceptance of all that the person is. In D-cognition, "perfection" implies necessarily mistaken perceiving and illusion. In the first sense, every living human being is perfect; in the second sense, no person is perfect, nor ever can be. That is to say, we may see him as B-perfect while he may think that we perceive him as D-perfect and, of course, may be made uncomfortable, unworthy and guilty thereby, as if he were fooling us.

We may reasonably deduce that the more capable a person is of B-cognition, the more he is able to accept and enjoy being B-cognized. We may also expect that the possibility of such misunderstanding may often pose a delicate problem of tactics upon the B-cognizer, the one who can totally understand and accept another.

8. *Possible over-estheticism is the last tactical problem entailed by B-cognition that I have space to speak of here.* The esthetic reaction to life often conflicts intrinsically with the practical and with the moral reaction to life (the old conflict between style and content). Depicting ugly things beautifully is one possibility. Another is the inept, unesthetic presentation of the true or the good or even the beautiful. (We leave aside the true-good-beautiful presentation of the true-good-beautiful as presenting no problem.) Since this dilemma has been much debated throughout history, I confine myself here merely to pointing out that it also involves the problem of social responsibility of the more mature for the less mature who may confuse B-acceptance with D-approval. A moving and beautiful presentation of, e.g., homosexuality or crime or irresponsibility, arising out of deep understanding, may be misunderstood as inciting to emulation. For the B-cognizer who lives in a world of frightened and easily misled people, this is an additional burden of responsibility to bear.

Empirical Findings

What has been the relation between B-cognition and D-cognition in my self-actualizing subjects (97)? How have they related contemplation to action? Though these questions did not occur to me at the time in this form, I can report retrospectively the following impressions. First of all, these subjects were far more capable of B-cognition and pure contemplation and understanding than the average population, as stated at the outset. This seems to be a matter of degree, since everyone seems to be capable of occasional B-cognition, pure contemplation, peak-experience, etc. Secondly, they were also uniformly more capable of effective action and D-cognition. It must be admitted that this may be an epiphenomenon of selecting subjects in the United States; or even that it may be a by-product of the fact that the selector of the subjects was an American. In any case I must report that I ran across no Buddhist-monk-like people in my searches. Thirdly, my retrospective impression is that the most fully-human people, a good deal of the time, live what we could call an ordinary life—shopping, eating, being polite, going to the dentist, thinking of money, meditating profoundly over a choice between black shoes or brown shoes, going to silly movies, reading ephemeral literature. They may be expected ordinarily to be annoyed with bores, to be shocked by misdeeds, etc., even though this reaction may be less intense, or more tinged by compassion. Peak-experiences, B-cognitions, pure contemplation, whatever their relative frequency may be, seem, in terms of absolute numbers, to be exceptional experiences even for self-actualizing people. This seems true even though it is also true that more matured people live all or most of the time at a higher level in some other ways, e.g., more clearly differentiating means from ends, profound from superficial; being generally more perspicuous, more spontaneous and expressive, more profoundly related to the ones they love, etc.

Therefore the problem posed here is more an ultimate than an immediate one, more a theoretical problem than a practical one. And yet these dilemmas are important for more than the theoretical effort to define the possibilities and the limits of human nature. Because they are also breeders of real guilt, of real conflict, of what we might also call "real existential psychopathology," we must continue to struggle with them as personal problems as well.

Resistance to Being Rubricized

"Resistance" in the Freudian conceptual system refers to the maintenance of repressions. But Schachtel (147) has already shown that difficulties in the coming to consciousness of ideas may have other sources than repression. Some kinds of awareness which were possible for the child may be said simply to have been "forgotten" in the course of growing up. I, too, have attempted to make a differentiation between the weaker resistance to unconscious primary-process cognitions and the very much stronger resistance to forbidden impulses, drives or wishes (100). These developments, and others, indicate that it may be desirable to expand the concept "resistance" to mean approximately "difficulties in achieving insight for *whatever* reason" (excluding of course constitutional incapacity, e.g., feeblemindedness, reduction to the concrete, gender differences, and perhaps even constitutional determinants of the Sheldon type).

The thesis here is that another source of "resistance" in the therapeutic situation can be a healthy distaste by the patient for being rubricized or casually classified, i.e., for being deprived of his individuality, his uniqueness, his differences from all others, his special identity.

I have previously (97, Chapter 14) described rubricizing as a cheap form of cognizing, i.e., really a form of not-cognizing, a quick, easy cataloguing whose function is to make unnecessary the effort required by more careful, idiographic perceiving or thinking. To place a person in a system takes less energy than to know him in his own right, since in the former instance, all that has to be perceived is that one abstracted characteristic which indicates his belongingness in a class, e.g., babies, waiters, Swedes, schizophrenics, females, generals, nurses, etc. What is stressed in rubricizing is the category in which the person belongs, of which he is a sample, not the person as such —similarities rather than differences.

In this same publication, the very important fact was noted that being rubricized is generally offensive to the person rubricized, since it denies his individuality or pays no attention to his personhood, to his differential, unique identity. William James's famous statement in 1902 makes the point clear:

"The first thing the intellect does with an object is to class it with something else. But any object that is infinitely important to us and awakens our devotion feels to us also as if it must be *sui generis* and unique. Probably a crab would be filled with a sense of personal outrage if it could hear us class it without ado or apology as a crustacean, and thus dispose of it. 'I am no such thing,' it would say; 'I am *myself, myself* alone' (70a, p. 10).

One illustrative example of the resentment elicited by being rubricized may be cited from a current study by the author on conceptions of masculinity and femininity in Mexico and in the United States (105). Most American women, after their first adjustment to Mexico, find it very pleasant to be valued so highly as females, to create a turmoil of whistling and sighing wherever they go, to be sought out eagerly by men of all ages, to be regarded as beautiful and as valuable. For many American women, ambivalent as they often are about their femininity, this can be a very satisfying and therapeutic experience, making them feel more female, more ready to enjoy femininity, which in turn makes them often *look* more feminine.

But as time goes on, they (some of them, at least) find this less pleasing. They discover that *any* woman is valuable to the Mexican male, that there seems to be little discrimination between old and young women, beautiful and not beautiful, intelligent and not intelligent. Furthermore, they find that in contrast with the young American male (who, as one girl put it, "gets so traumatized when you refuse to go out with him that he has to go to his psychiatrist"), the Mexican male takes a refusal very calmly, *too* calmly. He does not seem to mind and quickly turns to another woman. But this means then to a specific woman that *she*, she herself, as a person, is not specially valuable to him, and that all his efforts were directed toward a *woman*, not toward *her*, which implies that one woman is about as good as another, and that she is interchangeable with others. She discovers that *she* is not valuable; it is the class "woman" that is valuable. And finally she feels insulted rather than flattered, since she wants to be valued as a person, for *herself*, rather than for her gender. Of course, femalehood is prepotent over personhood, i.e., it calls for prior gratification, yet its gratification brings the claims of personhood into the foreground of the motivational economy. Enduring romantic love, monogamy and the self-actualization of women are all made possible by regard for a particular person rather than for the class, "woman."

Another very common example of the resentment to being rubricized is the rage so commonly aroused in adolescents when they are told, "Oh that's just a stage you're going through. You'll grow out of it eventually." What is tragic and real and unique to the child cannot be laughed at even though it has happened and will happen to millions of others.

One final illustration: a psychiatrist terminated a very brief and hurried first interview with a prospective patient by saying, "Your troubles are roughly those characteristic of your age." The potential patient became very angry and later reported feeling "brushed off" and insulted. She felt as if she had been treated like a child: "I am *not* a specimen. I'm *me*, not anybody else."

Considerations of this sort can also help us to expand our notion of resistance in classical psychoanalysis. Because resistance is customarily treated as *only* a defense of the neurosis, as a resistance to getting well or to perceiving unpleasant truths, it is therefore often treated as something undesirable, something to overcome and to analyze away. But as the examples above have indicated, what has been treated as sickness *may* sometimes be health, or at least not sickness. The therapist's difficulties with his patients, their refusal to accept an interpretation, their anger and fighting back, their stubbornness, almost surely, in *some* cases, arises from a refusal to be rubricized. Such resistance may therefore be seen as an assertion of and protection of personal uniqueness, identity or selfhood against attack or neglect. Such reactions not only maintain the dignity of the individual; they also serve to protect him against bad psychotherapy, textbook interpretation, "wild analysis," overintellectual or premature interpretations or explanations, meaningless abstractions or conceptualizations, all of which imply to the patient a lack of respect; for a similar treatment, see O'Connell (129).

Novices at therapy in their eagerness to cure quickly, "textbook boys" who memorize a conceptual system and then conceive of therapy as no more than passing out concepts, theorists without clinical experience, the undergraduate or graduate student in psychology who has just memorized Fenichel and is willing to tell everyone in the dormitory what category he belongs in—these are the rubricizers against whom patients have to protect themselves. These are the ones who pass out easily and quickly, perhaps even on first contact, such statements as, "You are an anal character," or, "You're just trying to dominate everyone," or, "You want me to sleep with you," or "You really want your father to give you a baby," etc.[14] To call the legitimate self-protective reaction against such rubricizing "resistance" in the classical sense is then just another example of the misuse of a concept.

Fortunately, there are indications of a reaction against rubricizing among those responsible for the treatment of people. One sees this in the general turning away from taxonomical, "Kraepelinian," or "state hospital" psychiatry by enlightened therapists. The main effort, sometimes the *only* effort, used to be diagnosis, i.e., placing the individual within a class. But experience has taught that diagnosis is more a legal and administrative necessity than a therapeutic one. Now, even in psychiatric hospitals, it has become increasingly recognized that nobody is a textbook patient; diagnostic statements in staff meetings are getting longer, richer, more complex, less a simple labeling.

The patient, it is now realized, must be approached as a single, unique person rather than as a member of a class—that is, if the main purpose is psychotherapy. Understanding a person is not the same as classifying or rubricizing him. And understanding a person is the *sine qua non* for therapy.

Summary

Human beings often resent being rubricized, which can be seen by them as a denial of their individuality (self, identity). They may be expected to react by reaffirming their identity in the various ways open to them. In psychotherapy, such reactions must be sympathetically understood as affirmations of personal dignity, which in *any* case is under severe assault in some forms of therapy. Either such self-protective reactions ought not to be called "resistance" (in the sense of a sickness-protecting maneuver), or else the concept "resistance" must be expanded to include many kinds of difficulty in achieving awareness. It is furthermore pointed out that such resistances are extremely valuable protectors against bad psychotherapy.[15]

Part IV

Creativeness

Creativity in Self-Actualizing People

I first had to change my ideas about creativity as soon as I began studying people who were positively healthy, highly evolved and matured, self-actualizing. I had first to give up my stereotyped notion that health, genius, talent and productivity were synonymous. A fair proportion of my subjects, though healthy and creative in a special sense that I am going to describe, were *not* productive in the ordinary sense, nor did they have great talent or genius, nor were they poets, composers, inventors, artists or creative intellectuals. It was also obvious that some of the greatest talents of mankind were certainly not psychologically healthy people, Wagner, for example, or Van Gogh or Byron. Some were and some weren't, it was clear. I very soon had to come to the conclusion that great talent was not only more or less independent of goodness or health of character but also that we know little about it. For instance, there is some evidence that great musical talent and mathematical talent are more inherited than acquired (150). It seemed clear then that health and special talent were separate variables, maybe only slightly correlated, maybe not. We may as well admit at the beginning that psychology knows very little about special talent of the genius type. I shall say nothing more about it, confining myself instead to that more widespread kind of creativeness which is the universal heritage of every human being that is born, and which seems to co-vary with psychological health.

Furthermore, I soon discovered that I had, like most other people, been thinking of creativeness in terms of products, and secondly, I had unconsciously confined creativeness to certain conventional areas only of human endeavor, unconsciously assuming that *any* painter, *any* poet, *any* composer was leading a creative life. Theorists, artists, scientists, inventors, writers could be creative. Nobody else could be. Unconsciously I had assumed that creativeness was the prerogative solely of certain professionals.

But these expectations were broken up by various of my subjects. For instance, one woman, uneducated, poor, a full-time housewife and mother, did none of these conventionally creative things and yet was a marvellous cook, mother, wife and home-maker. With little money, her home was somehow always beautiful. She was a perfect hostess. Her meals were banquets. Her taste in linens, silver, glass, crockery and furniture was impeccable. She was in all these areas original, novel, ingenious, unexpected, inventive. I just *had* to call her creative. I learned from her and others like her that a first-rate soup is more creative than a second-rate painting, and that, generally, cooking or parenthood or making a home could be creative while poetry need not be; it could be uncreative.

Another of my subjects devoted herself to what had best be called social service in the broadest sense, bandaging up wounds, helping the downtrodden, not only in a personal way, but in an organizational way as well. One of her "creations" is an organization which helps many more people than she could individually.

Another was a psychiatrist, a "pure" clinician who never wrote anything or created any theories or researches but who delighted in his everyday job of helping people to create themselves. This man approached each patient as if he were the only one in the world, without jargon, expectations or presuppositions, with innocence and naivete and yet with great wisdom, in a Taoistic fashion. Each patient was a unique human being and therefore a completely new problem to be understood and solved in a completely novel way. His great success even with very difficult cases validated his "creative" (rather than stereotyped or orthodox) way of doing things. From another man I learned that constructing a business organization could be a creative activity. From a young athlete, I learned that a perfect tackle could be as esthetic a product as a sonnet and could be approached in the same creative spirit. In other words, I learned to apply the word "creative" (and also the word "esthetic") not only to products but also to people in a characterological way, and to activities, processes, and attitudes. And furthermore, I had come to apply the word "creative" to many products other than the standard and conventionally accepted poems, theories, novels, experiments or paintings.

The consequence was that I found it necessary to distinguish "special talent creativeness" from "self-actualizing (SA) creativeness" which sprang much more directly from the personality, and which showed itself widely in the ordinary affairs of life, for instance, in a certain kind of humor. It looked like a tendency to do *anything* creatively: e.g., housekeeping, teaching, etc. Frequently, it appeared that an essential aspect of SA creativeness was a special kind of perceptiveness that is exemplified by the child in the fable who saw that the king had no clothes on this too contradicts the notion of creativity as products . Such people can see the fresh, the raw, the concrete, the ideographic, as well as the generic, the abstract, the rubricized, the categorized and the classified. Consequently, they live far more in the real world of nature than in the verbalized world of concepts, abstractions, expectations, beliefs and stereotypes that most people confuse with the real world (97, Chapter 14). This is well expressed in Rogers' phrase "openness to experience" (145).

All my subjects were relatively more spontaneous and expressive than average people. They were more "natural" and less controlled and inhibited in their behavior, which seemed to flow out more easily and freely and with less blocking and self-criticism. This ability to express ideas and impulses without strangulation and without fear of ridicule turned out to be an essential aspect of SA creativeness. Rogers has used the excellent phrase, "fully functioning person," to describe this aspect of health (145).

Another observation was that SA creativeness was in many respects like the creativeness of *all* happy and secure children. It was spontaneous, effortless, innocent, easy, a kind of freedom from stereotypes and cliches. And again it seemed to be made up largely of "innocent" freedom of perception, and "innocent," uninhibited spontaneity and expressiveness. Almost any child can perceive more freely, without a priori expectations about what ought to be there, what must be there, or what has always been there. And almost any child can compose a song or a poem or a dance or a painting or a play or a game on the spur of the moment, without planning or previous intent.

It was in this childlike sense that my subjects were creative. Or to avoid misunderstanding, since my subjects were after all not children (they were all people in their 50's or 60's), let us say that they had either retained or regained at least these two main aspects of childlikeness, namely, they were non-rubricizing or "open to experience" and they were easily spontaneous and expressive. If children are naive, then my subjects had attained a "second naivete," as Santayana called it. Their innocence of perception and expressiveness was combined with sophisticated minds.

In any case, this all sounds as if we are dealing with a fundamental characteristic, inherent in human nature, a potentiality given to all or most human beings at birth, which most often is lost or buried or inhibited as the person gets enculturated.

My subjects were different from the average person in another characteristic that makes creativity more likely. SA people are relatively unfrightened by the unknown, the mysterious, the puzzling, and often are positively attracted by it, i.e., selectively pick it out to puzzle over, to meditate on and to be absorbed with. I quote from my description (97, p. 206): "They do not neglect the unknown, or deny it, or run away from it, or try to make believe it is really known, nor do they organize, dichotomize, or rubricize it prematurely. They do not cling to the familiar, nor is their quest for the truth a catastrophic need for certainty, safety, definiteness, and order, such as we see in an exaggerated form in Goldstein's brain injured or in the compulsive-obsessive neurotic. They can be, when the total objective situation calls for it, comfortably disorderly, sloppy, anarchic, chaotic, vague, doubtful, uncertain, indefinite, approximate, inexact, or inaccurate (all at certain moments in science, art, or life in general, quite desirable).

"Thus it comes about that doubt, tentativeness, uncertainty, with the consequent necessity for abeyance of decision, which is for most a torture, can be for some a pleasantly stimulating challenge, a high spot in life rather than a low."

One observation I made has puzzled me for many years but it begins to fall into place now. It was what I described as the resolution of dichotomies in self-actualizing people. Briefly stated, I found that I had to see differently many oppositions and polarities that all psychologists had taken for granted as straight line continua. For instance, to take the first dichotomy that I had trouble with, I couldn't decide whether my subjects were selfish or unselfish. (Observe how spontaneously we fall into an either-or, here. The more of one, the less of the other, is the implication of the style in which I put the question). But I was forced by sheer pressure of fact to give up this Aristotelian style of logic. My subjects were very unselfish in one sense and very selfish in another sense. And the two fused together, not like incompatibles, but rather in a sensible, dynamic unity or synthesis very much like what Fromm has described in his classical paper on healthy selfishness (50). My subjects had put opposites together in such a way as to make me realize that regarding selfishness and unselfishness as contradictory and mutually exclusive is itself characteristic of a lower level of personality development. So also in my subjects were many other dichotomies resolved into unities, cognition vs. conation (heart vs. head, wish vs. fact) became cognition "structured with" conation as instinct and reason came to the same conclusions. Duty became pleasure, and pleasure merged with duty. The distinction between work and play became shadowy. How could selfish hedonism be opposed to altruism, when altruism became selfishly pleasurable? These most mature of all people were also strongly childlike. These same people, the strongest egos ever described and the most definitely individual, were also precisely the ones who could be most easily egoless, self-transcending, and problem-centered (97, pp. 232-34).

But this is precisely what the great artist does. He is able to bring together clashing colors, forms that fight each other, dissonances of all kinds, into a unity. And this is also what the great theorist does when he puts puzzling and inconsistent facts together so that we can see that they really belong together. And so also for the great statesman, the great therapist, the great philosopher, the great parent, the great inventor. They are all integrators, able to bring separates and even opposites together into unity.

We speak here of the ability to integrate and of the play back and forth between integration within the person, and his ability to integrate whatever it is he is doing in the world. To the extent that creativeness is constructive, synthesizing, unifying, and integrative, to that extent does it depend in part on the inner integration of the person.

In trying to figure out why all this was so, it seemed to me that much of it could be traced back to the relative absence of fear in my subjects. They were certainly less enculturated; that is, they seemed to be less afraid of what other people would say or demand or laugh at. They had less need of other people and therefore, depending on them less, could be less afraid of them and less hostile against them. Perhaps more important, however, was their lack of fear of their own insides, of their own impulses, emotions, thoughts. They were more self-accepting than the average. This approval and acceptance of their deeper selves then made it more possible to perceive bravely the real nature of the world and also made their behavior more spontaneous (less controlled, less inhibited, less planned, less "willed" and designed). They were less afraid of their own thoughts even when they were "nutty" or silly or crazy. They were less afraid of being laughed at or of being disapproved of. They could let themselves be flooded by emotion. In contrast, average and neurotic people wall off through fear, much that lies within themselves. They control, they inhibit, they repress, and they suppress. They disapprove of their deeper selves and expect that others do, too.

What I am saying in effect is that the creativity of my subjects seemed to be an epiphenomenon of their greater wholeness and integration, which is what self-acceptance implies. The civil war within the average person between the forces of the inner depths and the forces of defense and control seems to have been resolved in my subjects and they are less split. As a consequence, more of themselves is available for use, for enjoyment and for creative purposes. They waste less of their time and energy protecting themselves against themselves.

As we have seen in previous chapters, what we know of peak-experiences supports and enriches these conclusions. These too are integrated and integrating experiences which are to some extent, isomorphic with integration in the perceived world. In these experiences also, we find increased openness to experience, and increased spontaneity and expressiveness. Also, since one aspect of this integration within the person is the acceptance and greater availability of our deeper selves, these deep roots of creativeness (84) become more available for use.

Primary, Secondary, and Integrated Creativeness

Classical Freudian theory is of little use for our purposes and is even partially contradicted by our data. It is (or was) essentially an id psychology, an investigation of the instinctive impulses and their vicissitudes, and the basic Freudian dialectic is seen to be ultimately between impulses and defenses against them. But far more crucial than repressed impulses for understanding the sources of creativity (as well as play, love, enthusiasm, humor, imagination, and fantasy) are the so-called primary processes which are essentially cognitive rather than conative. As soon as we turn our attention to this aspect of human depth-psychology, we find much agreement between the psychoanalytic ego-psychology—Kris (84), Milner (113), Ehrenzweig (39), the Jungian psychology (74), and the American self-and-growth psychology (118).

The normal adjustment of the average, common sense, well-adjusted man implies a continued successful rejection of much of the depths of human nature, both conative and cognitive. To adjust well to the world of reality means a splitting of the person. It means that the person turns his back on much in himself because it is dangerous. But it is now clear that by so doing, he loses a great deal too, for these depths are also the source of all his joys, his ability to play, to love, to laugh, and, most important for us, to be creative. By protecting himself against the hell within himself, he also cuts himself off from the heaven within. In the extreme instance, we have the obsessional person, flat, tight, rigid, frozen, controlled, cautious, who can't laugh or play or love, or be silly or trusting or childish. His imagination, his intuitions, his softness, his emotionality tend to be strangulated or distorted.

The goals of psychoanalysis as a therapy are ultimately integrative. The effort is to heal this basic split by insight, so that what has been repressed becomes conscious or preconscious. But here again we can make modifications as a consequence of studying the depth sources of creativeness. Our relation to our primary processes is not in all respects the same as our relation to unacceptable wishes. The most important difference that I can see is that our primary processes are not as dangerous as the forbidden impulses. To a large extent they are not repressed or censored but rather are "forgotten," or else turned away from, suppressed (rather than repressed), as we have to adjust to a harsh reality which demands a purposeful and pragmatic striving rather than revery, poetry, play. Or, to say it in another way, in a rich society there must be far less resistance to primary thought processes. I expect that education processes, which are known to do rather little for relieving repression of "instinct," can do much to accept and integrate the primary processes into conscious and preconscious life. Education in art, poetry, dancing, can in principle do much in this direction. And so also can education in dynamic psychology; for instance, Deutsch and Murphy's "Clinical Interview," which speaks in primary process language (38), can be seen as a kind of poetry. Marion Milner's extraordinary book, *On Not Being Able to Paint*, perfectly makes my point (113).

The kind of creativeness I have been trying to sketch out is best exemplified by the improvisation, as in jazz or in childlike paintings, rather than by the work of art designated as "great."

In the first place, the great work needs great talent which, as we have seen, turned out to be irrelevant for our concern. In the second place, the great work needs not only the flash, the inspiration, the peak-experience; it also needs hard work, long training, unrelenting criticism, perfectionistic standards. In other words, succeeding upon the spontaneous is the deliberate; succeeding upon total acceptance comes criticism; succeeding upon intuition comes rigorous thought; succeeding upon daring comes caution; succeeding upon fantasy and imagination comes reality testing. Now come the questions, "Is it true?" "Will it be understood by the other?" "Is its structure sound?" "Does it stand the test of logic?" "How will it do in the world?" "Can I prove it?" Now come the comparisons, the judgments, the evaluations, the cold, calculating morning-after thoughts, the selections and the rejections.

If I may say it so, the secondary processes now take over from the primary, the Apollonian from the Dionysian, the "masculine" from the "feminine." The voluntary regression into our depths is now terminated, the necessary passivity and receptivity of inspiration or of peak-experience must now give way to activity, control, and hard work. A peak-experience happens *to* a person, but the person *makes* the great product.

Strictly speaking, I have investigated this first phase only, that which comes easily and without effort as a spontaneous expression of an integrated person, or of a transient unifying within the person. It can come only if a person's depths are available to him, only if he is not afraid of his primary thought processes.

I shall call "primary creativity" that which proceeds from and uses the primary process much more than the secondary processes. The creativity which is based mostly on the secondary thought processes I shall call "secondary creativity." This latter type includes a large proportion of production-in-the-world, the bridges, the houses, the new automobiles, even many scientific experiments and much literary work. All of these are essentially the consolidation and development of other people's ideas. It parallels the difference between the commando and the military policeman behind the lines, between the pioneer and the settler. That creativity which uses *both* types of process easily and well, in good fusion or in good succession, I shall call "integrated creativity." It is from this kind that comes the great work of art, or philosophy, or science.

Conclusion

The upshot of all of these developments can, I think, be summarized as an increased stress on the role of integration (or self-consistency, unity, wholeness) in the theory of creativeness. Resolving a dichotomy into a higher, more inclusive, unity amounts to healing a split in the person and making him more unified. Since the splits I have been talking about are within the person, they amount to a kind of civil war, a setting of one part of the person against another part. In any case so far as SA creativeness is concerned, it seems to come more immediately from fusion of primary and secondary processes rather than from working through repressive control of forbidden impulses and wishes. It is, of course, probable that defenses arising out of fears of these forbidden impulses also push down primary processes in a kind of total, undiscriminating, panicky war on *all* the depths. But it seems that such lack of discrimination is not in principle necessary.

To summarize, SA creativeness stresses first the personality rather than its achievements, considering these achievements to be epiphenomena emitted by the personality and therefore secondary to it. It stresses characterological qualities like boldness, courage, freedom, spontaneity, perspicuity, integration, self-acceptance, all of which make possible the kind of generalized SA creativeness, which expresses itself in the creative life, or the creative attitude, or the creative person. I have also stressed the expressive or Being quality of SA creativeness rather than its problem-solving or product-making quality. SA creativeness is "emitted," like radioactivity, and hits all of life, regardless of problems, just as a cheerful person "emits" cheerfulness without purpose or design or even consciousness. It is emitted like sunshine; it spreads all over the place; it makes some things grow (which are growable) and is wasted on rocks and other ungrowable things.

Finally, I am quite aware that I have been trying to break up widely accepted concepts of creativity without being able to offer in exchange a nice, clearly defined, clean-cut substitute concept. SA creativeness is hard to define because sometimes it seems to be synonymous with health itself, as Moustakas (118) has suggested. And since self-actualization or health must ultimately be defined as the coming to pass of the fullest humanness, or as the "Being" of the person, it is as if SA creativity were almost synonymous with, or a *sine qua non* aspect of, or a defining characteristic of, essential humanness.

Part V

Values

Psychological Data and Human Values

Humanists for thousands of years have attempted to construct a naturalistic, psychological value system that could be derived from man's own nature, without the necessity of recourse to authority outside the human being himself. Many such theories have been offered throughout history. They have all failed for mass practical purposes exactly as all other theories have failed. We have about as many scoundrels in the world today as we have ever had, and *many more* neurotics, probably, than we have ever had.

These inadequate theories, most of them, rested on psychological assumptions of one sort or another. Today practically all of these can be shown, in the light of recently acquired knowledge, to be false, inadequate, incomplete or in some other way, lacking. But it is my belief that certain developments in the science and art of psychology, in the last few decades, make it possible for us for the first time to feel confident that this age-old hope may be fulfilled if only we work hard enough. We know how to criticize the old theories; we know, even though dimly, the shape of the theories to come, and most of all, we know where to look and what to do in order to fill in the gaps in knowledge, that will permit us to answer the age-old questions, "What is the good life? What is the good man? How can people be taught to desire and prefer the good life? How ought children to be brought up to be sound adults? etc." That is, we think that a scientific ethic may be possible, and we think we know how to go about constructing it.

The following section will discuss briefly a few of the promising lines of evidence and of research, their relevance to past and future value theories, along with a discussion of the theoretical and factual advances we must make in the near future. It is safer to judge them all as more or less probable rather than as certain.

Free Choice Experiments: Homeostasis

Hundreds of experiments have been made that demonstrate a universal inborn ability in all sorts of animals to select a beneficial diet if enough alternatives are presented from among which they are permitted free choice. This wisdom of the body is often retained under less usual conditions, e.g., adrenalectomized animals can keep themselves alive by readjusting their self-chosen diet. Pregnant animals will nicely adjust their diets to the needs of the growing embryo.

We now know this is by no means a perfect wisdom. These appetites are less efficient, for instance, in reflecting body need for vitamins. Lower animals protect themselves against poisons more efficiently than higher animals and humans. Previously formed habits of preference may quite overshadow present metabolic needs (185). And most of all, in the human being, and especially in the neurotic human being, all sorts of forces can contaminate this wisdom of the body, although it never seems to be lost altogether.

The general principle is true not only for selection of food but also for all sorts of other body needs as the famous homeostasis experiments have shown (27).

It seems quite clear that all organisms are more self-governing, self-regulating and autonomous than we thought 25 years ago. The organism deserves a good deal of trust, and we are learning steadily to rely on this internal wisdom of our babies with reference to choice of diet, time of weaning, amount of sleep, time of toilet training, need for activity, and a lot else.

But more recently we have been learning, especially from physically and mentally sick people, that there are good choosers and bad choosers. We have learned, especially from the psychoanalysts, much about the hidden causes of such behavior and have learned to respect these causes.

In this connection we have available a startling experiment (38 b), which is pregnant with implications for value theory. Chickens allowed to choose their own diet vary widely in their ability to choose what is good for them. The good choosers become stronger, larger, more dominant than the poor choosers, which means that they get the best of everything. If then the diet chosen by the good choosers is forced upon the poor choosers, it is found that *they* now get stronger, bigger, healthier and more dominant, although never reaching the level of the good choosers. That is, good choosers can choose better than bad choosers what is better for the bad choosers themselves. If similar experimental findings are made in human beings, as I think they will be (supporting clinical data are available aplenty), we are in for a good deal of reconstruction of all sorts of theories. So far as human value theory is concerned, no theory will be adequate that rests simply on the statistical description of the choices of un-selected human beings. To average the choices of good and bad choosers, of healthy and sick people is useless. Only the choices and tastes and judgments of healthy human beings will tell us much about what is good for the human species in the long run. The choices of neurotic people can tell us mostly what is good for keeping a neurosis stabilized, just as the choices of a brain injured man are good for preventing a catastrophic breakdown, or as the choices of an adrenalectomized animal may keep *him* from dying but would kill a healthy animal.

I think that this is the main reef on which most hedonistic value theories and ethical theories have foundered. Pathologically motivated pleasures cannot be averaged with healthily motivated pleasures.

Furthermore any ethical code will have to deal with the fact of constitutional differences not only in chickens and rats but also in men, as Sheldon (153) and Morris (110) have shown. Some values are common to all (healthy) mankind, but also some other values will *not* be common to all mankind, but only to some types of people, or to specific individuals. What I have called the basic needs are probably common to all mankind and are, therefore, shared values. But idiosyncratic needs generate idiosyncratic values.

Constitutional differences in individuals generate preferences among ways of relating to self, and to culture and to the world, i.e., generate values. These researches support and are supported by the universal experience of clinicians with individual differences. This is also true of the ethnological data that make sense of cultural diversity by postulating that each culture selects for exploitation, suppression, approval or disapproval, a small segment of the range of human constitutional possibilities. This is all in line with the biological data and theories and self-actualization theories which show that an organ system presses to express itself, in a word, to function. The muscular person likes to use his muscles, indeed, *has* to use them in order to self-actualize, and to achieve the subjective feeling of harmonious, uninhibited, satisfying functioning which is so important an aspect of psychological health. People with intelligence must use their intelligence, people with eyes must use their eyes, people with the capacity to love have the *impulse* to love and the *need* to love in order to feel healthy. Capacities clamor to be used, and cease their clamor only when they *are* used sufficiently. That is to say, capacities are needs, and therefore are intrinsic values as well. To the extent that capacities differ, so will values also differ.

Basic Needs and Their Hierarchical Arrangement

It has by now been sufficiently demonstrated that the human being has, as part of his intrinsic construction, not only physiological needs, but also truly psychological ones. They may be considered as deficiencies which must be optimally fulfilled by the environment in order to avoid sickness and subjective ill-being. They can be called basic, or biological, and likened to the need for salt, or calcium or vitamin D because—

a) The deprived person yearns for their gratification persistently.
b) Their deprivation makes the person sicken and wither.
c) Gratifying them is therapeutic, curing the deficiency-illness.
d) Steady supplies forestall these illnesses.
e) Healthy (gratified) people do not demonstrate these deficiencies.

But these needs or values are related to each other in a hierarchical and developmental way, in an order of strength and of priority. Safety is a more prepotent, or stronger, more pressing, more vital need than love, for instance, and the need for food is usually stronger than either. Furthermore, *all* these basic needs may be considered to be simply steps along the path to general self-actualization, under which all basic needs can be subsumed.

By taking these data into account, we can solve many value problems that philosophers have struggled with ineffectually for centuries. For one thing, it looks as if *there were* a single ultimate value for mankind, a far goal toward which all men strive. This is called variously by different authors self-actualization, self-realization, integration, psychological health, individuation, autonomy, creativity, productivity, but they all agree that this amounts to realizing the potentialities of the person, that is to say, becoming fully human, everything that the person *can* become.

But it is also true that the person himself does not know this. We, the psychologists observing and studying, have constructed this concept in order to integrate and explain lots of diverse data. So far as the person himself is concerned, all *he* knows is that he is desperate for love, and thinks he will be forever happy and content if he gets it. He does not know in advance that he will strive on *after* this gratification has come, and that gratification of one basic need opens consciousness to domination by another, "higher" need. So far as he is concerned, *the* absolute, ultimate value, synonymous with life itself, is whichever need in the hierarchy he is dominated by during a particular period. These basic needs or basic values therefore may be treated *both* as ends and as steps toward a single end-goal. It is true that there is a single, ultimate value or end of life and *also* it is just as true that we have a hierarchical and developmental system of values, complexly interrelated.

This also helps to solve the apparent paradox of contrast between Being and Becoming. It is true that human beings strive perpetually toward ultimate humanness, which itself may be anyway a different kind of Becoming and growing. It's as if we were doomed forever to try to arrive at a state to which we could never attain. Fortunately we now know this not to be true, or at least it is not the only truth. There is another truth which integrates with it. We are again and again rewarded for good Becoming by transient states of absolute Being, by peak-experiences. Achieving basic-need gratifications gives us many peak-experiences, each of which are absolute delights, perfect in themselves, and needing no more than themselves to validate life. This is like rejecting the notion that a Heaven lies someplace beyond the end of the path of life. Heaven, so to speak, lies waiting for us through life, ready to step into for a time and to enjoy before we have to come back to our ordinary life of striving. And once we have been in it, we can remember it forever, and feed ourselves on this memory and be sustained in time of stress.

Not only this, but the process of moment-to-moment growth is itself intrinsically rewarding and delightful in an absolute sense. If they are not mountain peak-experiences, at least they are foothill-experiences, little glimpses of absolute, self-validative delight, little moments of Being. Being and Becoming are *not* contradictory or mutually exclusive. Approaching and arriving are both in themselves rewarding.

I should make it clear here that I want to differentiate the Heaven ahead (of growth and transcendence) from the "Heaven" behind (of regression). The "high Nirvana" is quite different from the "low Nirvana" even though most clinicians confuse them (see also 170).

Self-Actualization: Growth

I have published in another place a survey of all the evidence that forces us in the direction of a concept of healthy growth or of self-actualizing tendencies (97). This is partly deductive evidence in the sense of pointing out that unless we postulate such a concept, much of human behavior makes no sense. This is on the same scientific principle that led to the discovery of a hitherto unseen planet that *had* to be there in order to make sense of a lot of other observed data.

There is also some direct evidence, or rather the beginnings of direct evidence, which needs much more research to get to the point of certainty. The only direct study of self-actualizing people I know is the one I made, and it is a very shaky business to rest on just one study made by just one person when we take into account the known pitfalls of sampling error, of projection, etc. However, the conclusions of this study have been so strongly paralleled in the clinical and philosophical conclusions of Rogers, Fromm, Goldstein, Angyal, Murray, Moustakas, C. Buhler, Horney, Jung, Nuttin and many others that I shall proceed under the assumption that more careful research will not contradict my findings radically. We can certainly now assert that at least a reasonable, theoretical, and empirical case has been made for the presence within the human being of a tendency toward, or need for growing in a direction that can be summarized in general as self-actualization, or psychological health, and specifically as growth toward each and all of the sub-aspects of self-actualization, i.e., he has within him a pressure toward unity of personality, toward spontaneous expressiveness, toward full individuality and identity, toward seeing the truth rather than being blind, toward being creative, toward being good, and a lot else. That is, the human being is so constructed that he presses toward fuller and fuller being and this means pressing toward what most people would call good values, toward serenity, kindness, courage, honesty, love, unselfishness, and goodness.

Few in number though they be, we can learn a great deal about values from the direct study of these highly evolved, most mature, psychologically healthiest individuals, and from the study of the peak moments of average individuals, moments in which they become transiently self-actualized. This is because they are in very real empirical and theoretical ways, most fully human. For instance, they are people who have retained and developed their human capacities, especially those capacities which define the human being and differentiate him from, let us say, the monkey. (This accords with Hartman's (59) axiological approach to the same problem of defining the good human being as the one who has more of the characteristics which define the concept "human being.") From a developmental point of view, they are more fully evolved because not fixated at immature or incomplete levels of growth. This is no more mysterious, or a priori, or question begging than the selection of a type specimen of butterfly by a taxonomist or the most physically healthy young man by the physician. They both look for the "perfect or mature or magnificent specimen" for the exemplar, and so have I. One procedure is as repeatable in principle as the other.

Full humanness can be defined not only in terms of the degree to which the definition of the concept "human" is fulfilled, i.e., the species norm. It also has a descriptive, cataloguing, measurable, psychological definition. We now have from a few research beginnings and from countless clinical experiences some notion of the characteristics both of the fully evolved human being and of the well-growing human being. These characteristics are not only neutrally describable; they are also subjectively rewarding, pleasurable and reinforcing.

Among the objectively describable and measurable characteristics of the healthy human specimen are—

1. Clearer, more efficient perception of reality.
2. More openness to experience.

3. Increased integration, wholeness, and unity of the person.
4. Increased spontaneity, expressiveness; full functioning; aliveness.
5. A real self; a firm identity; autonomy, uniqueness.
6. Increased objectivity, detachment, transcendence of self.
7. Recovery of creativeness.
8. Ability to fuse concreteness and abstractness.
9. Democratic character structure.
10. Ability to love, etc.

These all need research confirmation and exploration but it is clear that such researches are feasible.

In addition, there are subjective confirmations or reinforcements of self-actualization or of good growth toward it. These are the feelings of zest in living, of happiness or euphoria, of serenity, of joy, of calmness, of responsibility, of confidence in one's ability to handle stresses, anxieties, and problems. The subjective signs of self-betrayal, of fixation, of regression, and of living by fear rather than by growth are such feelings as anxiety, despair, boredom, inability to enjoy, intrinsic guilt, intrinsic shame, aimlessness, feelings of emptiness, of lack of identity, etc.

These subjective reactions are also susceptible of research exploration. We have clinical techniques available for studying them.

It is the free choices of such self-actualizing people (in those situations where real choice is possible from among a variety of possibilities) that I claim can be descriptively studied as a naturalistic value system with which the hopes of the observer absolutely have nothing to do, i.e., it is "scientific." I do not say, "He *ought* to choose this or that," but only, "Healthy people, permitted to choose freely, are *observed* to choose this or that." his is like asking, "What *are* the values of the best human beings," rather than, "What *should* be their values?" or, "What *ought* they be?" (Compare this with Aristotle's belief that "it is the things which are valuable and pleasant to a good man that are really valuable and pleasant.")

Furthermore, I think these findings can be generalized to most of the human species because it looks to me (and to others) as if most people (perhaps all) tend toward self-actualization (this is seen most clearly in the experiences in psychotherapy, especially of the uncovering sort), and as if, in principle at least, most people are *capable* of self-actualization.

If the various extant religions may be taken as expressions of human aspiration, i.e., what people would *like* to become if only they could, then we can see here too a validation of the affirmation that all people yearn toward self-actualization or tend toward it. This is so because our description of the actual characteristics of self-actualizing people parallels at many points the ideals urged by the religions, e.g., the transcendence of self, the fusion of the true, the good and the beautiful, contribution to others, wisdom, honesty and naturalness, the transcendence of selfish and personal motivations, the giving up of "lower" desires in favor of "higher" ones, the easy differentiation between ends (tranquilly, serenity, peace) and means (money, power, status), the decrease of hostility, cruelty and destructiveness and the increase of friendliness, kindness, etc.

1. One conclusion from all these free-choice experiments, from developments in dynamic motivation theory and from examination of psychotherapy, is a very revolutionary one that no other large culture had even arrived at, namely, that our deepest needs are *not*, in themselves, dangerous or evil or bad. This opens up the prospect of resolving the splits within the person between Apollonian and Dionysian, classical and romantic, scientific and poetic, between reason and impulse, work and play, verbal and preverbal, maturity and childlikeness, masculine and feminine, growth and regression.

2. The main social parallel to this change in our philosophy of human nature is the rapidly growing tendency to perceive the culture as an instrument of need-gratification as well as of frustration and control. We can now reject, as a localism, the almost universal mistake that the interests of the individual and of society are of *necessity* mutually exclusive and antagonistic, or that civilization is primarily a mechanism for controlling and policing human instinctoid impulses (93). All these age-old axioms are swept away by the new possibility of defining the main function of a healthy culture as the fostering of universal self-actualization.

3. In healthy people only is there a good correlation between subjective delight in the experience, impulse to the experience, or wish for it, and "basic need" for the experience (it's good for him in the long run). Only such people uniformly yearn for what is good for them and for others, and then are able wholeheartedly to enjoy it, and approve of it. For such people virtue is its own reward in the sense of being enjoyed in itself. They spontaneously tend to do right because that is what they *want* to do, what they *need* to do, what they enjoy, what they approve of doing, and what they will continue to enjoy.

It is this unity, this network of positive intercorrelation, that falls apart into separateness and conflict as the person gets psychologically sick. Then what he wants to do may be bad for him; even if he does it he may not enjoy it, even if he enjoys it, he may simultaneously disapprove of it, so that the enjoyment is itself poisoned or may disappear quickly. What he enjoys at first he may not enjoy later. His impulses, desires, and enjoyments then become a poor guide to living. He must accordingly mistrust and fear the impulses and the enjoyments which lead him astray, and so he is caught in conflict, dissociation, indecision; in a word, he is caught in civil war.

So far as philosophical theory is concerned, many historical dilemmas and contradictions are resolved by this finding. Hedonistic theory *does* work for healthy people; it does *not* work for sick people. The true, the good and the beautiful *do* correlate some, but only in healthy people do they correlate strongly.

4. Self-actualization is a relatively achieved "state of affairs" in a few people. In most people, however, it is rather a hope, a yearning, a drive, a "something" wished for but not yet achieved, showing itself clinically as drive toward health, integration, growth, etc. The projective tests are also able to detect these trends as potentialities rather than as overt behavior, just as an X-ray can detect incipient pathology before it has appeared on the surface.

This means for us that that which the person *is* and that which the person *could he* exist simultaneously for the psychologist, thereby resolving the dichotomy between Being and Becoming. Potentialities not only *will* be or could be; they also *are*. Self-actualization values as goals exist and are real even though not yet actualized. The human being is simultaneously that which he is and that which he yearns to be.

Growth and Environment

Man demonstrates *in his own nature* a pressure toward fuller and fuller Being, more and more perfect actualization of his humanness in exactly the same naturalistic, scientific sense that an acorn may be said to be "pressing toward" being an oak tree, or that a tiger can be observed to "push toward" being tigerish, or a horse toward being equine. Man is ultimately *not* molded or shaped into humanness, or taught to be human. The role of the environment is ultimately to permit him or help him to actualize *his own* potentialities, not *its* potentialities. The environment does not give him potentialities and capacities; he *has* them in inchoate or embryonic form, just exactly as he has embryonic arms and legs. And creativeness, spontaneity, selfhood, authenticity, caring for others, being able to love, yearning for truth are embryonic potentialities belonging to his species-membership just as much as are his arms and legs and brain and eyes.

This is not in contradiction to the data already amassed which show clearly that living in a family and in a culture are absolutely necessary to *actualize* these psychological potentials that define humanness. Let us avoid this confusion. A teacher or a culture doesn't create a human being. It doesn't implant within him the ability to love, or to be curious, or to philosophize, or to symbolize, or to be creative. Rather it permits, or fosters, or encourages or helps what exists in embryo to become real and actual. The same mother or the same culture, treating a kitten or a puppy in exactly the same way, cannot make it into a human being. The culture is sun and food and water: it is not the seed.

"Instinct" Theory

The group of thinkers who have been working with self-actualization, with self, with authentic humanness, etc., have pretty firmly established their case that man has a tendency to realize himself. By implication he is exhorted to be true to his own nature, to trust himself, to be authentic, spontaneous, honestly expressive, to look for the sources of his action in his own deep inner nature.

But, of course, this is an ideal counsel. They do not sufficiently warn that most adults don't know *how* to be authentic and that, if they "express" themselves, they may bring catastrophe not only upon themselves but upon others as well. What answer must be given to the rapist or the sadist who asks "Why should I too not trust and express myself?"

These thinkers as a group have been remiss in several respects. They have *implied* without making explicit that if you can behave authentically, you *will* behave well, that if you emit action from within, it will be good and right behavior. What is very clearly implied is that this innet core, this real self, is good, trustworthy, ethical. This is an affirmation that is clearly separable from the affirmation that man actualizes himself, and needs to be separately proven (as I think it will be). Furthermore, these writers have as a group very definitely ducked the crucial statement about this inner core, i.e., that it *must* in some degree be inherited or else everything else they say is so much hash.

In other words, we must grapple with "instinct" theory or, as I prefer to call it, basic need theory, that is to say, with the study of the original, intrinsic, in part heredity-determined needs, urges, wishes and, I may say, values of mankind. We can't play both the biology game and the sociology game simultaneously. We can't affirm *both* that culture does everything and anything, and that man has an inherent nature. The one is incompatible with the other.

And of all the problems in this area of instinct, the one of which we know least and should know most is that of aggression, hostility, hatred, and destructiveness. The Freudians claim this to be instinctive; most other dynamic psychologists claim it to be not directly instinctive, but rather an ever-present reaction to frustration of instinctoid or basic needs. The truth is that we don't really know. Clinical experience hasn't settled the problem because equally good clinicians come to these divergent conclusions. What we need is hard, firm research.

The Problems of Control and Limits

Another problem confronting the morals-from-within theorists is to account for the easy self-discipline which is customarily found in self-actualizing, authentic, genuine people and which is *not* found in average people.

In these healthy people we find duty and pleasure to be the same thing, as is also work and play, self-interest and altruism, individualism and selflessness. We know they *are* that way, but not how they *get* that way. I have the strong intuition that such authentic, fully human persons are the actualization of what many human beings could be. And yet we are confronted with the sad fact that so few people achieve this goal, perhaps only one in a hundred, or two hundred. We can be hopeful for mankind because in principle anybody *could* become a good and healthy man. But we must also feel sad because so few actually *do* become good men. If we wish to find out why some do and some don't, then the research problem presents itself of studying the life history of self-actualizing men to find out how they get that way.

We know already that the main prerequisite of healthy growth is gratification of the basic needs. (Neurosis is very often a deficiency disease, like avitaminosis.) But we have also learned that unbridled indulgence and gratification has its own dangerous consequences, e.g., psychopathic personality, "orality," irresponsibility, inability to bear stress, spoiling, immaturity, certain character disorders. Research findings are rare but there is now available a large store of clinical and educational experience which allows us to make a reasonable guess that the young child needs not only gratification; he needs also to learn the limitations that the physical world puts upon his gratifications, and he has to learn that other human beings seek for gratifications, too, even his mother and father, i.e., they are not only means to his ends. This means control, delay, limits, renunciation, frustration-tolerance and discipline. Only to the self-disciplined and responsible person can we say, "Do as you will, and it will probably be all right."

Regressive Forces: Psychopathology

We must also face squarely the problem of what stands in the way of growth; that is to say, the problems of cessation of growth and evasion of growth, of fixation, regression, and defensiveness, in a word the attractiveness of psychopathology, or as other people would prefer to say, the problem of evil.

Why do so many people have no real identity, so little power to make their own decisions and choices?

1. These impulses and directional tendencies towards self-fulfillment, though instinctive, are very weak, so that, in contrast with all other animals who have strong instincts, these impulses are very easily drowned out by habit, by wrong cultural attitudes toward them, by traumatic episodes, by erroneous education. Therefore, the problem of choice and of responsibility is far, far more acute in humans than in any other species.

2. There has been a special tendency in Western culture, historically determined, to assume that these instinctoid needs of the human being, his so-called animal nature, are bad or evil. As a consequence, many cultural institutions are set up for the express purpose of controlling, inhibiting, suppressing and repressing this original nature of man.

3. There are two sets of forces pulling at the individual, not just one. In addition to the pressures forward toward health, there are also fearful-regressive pressures backward, toward sickness and weakness. We can either move forward toward a "high Nirvana" or backward to a "low Nirvana."

I think the main factual defect in the value theories and ethical theories of the past and the present has been insufficient knowledge of psychopathology and psychotherapy. Throughout history, learned men have set out before mankind the rewards of virtue, the beauties of goodness, the intrinsic desirability of psychological health and self-fulfillment, and yet most people perversely refuse to step into the happiness and self-respect that is offered them. Nothing is left to the teachers but irritation, impatience, disillusionment, alternations between scolding, exhortation and hopelessness. A good many have thrown up their hands altogether and talked about original sin or intrinsic evil and concluded that man could be saved only by extra-human forces.

Meanwhile there lies available the huge, rich, and illuminating literature of dynamic psychology and psychopathology, a great store of information on man's weaknesses, and fears. We know much about *why* men do wrong things, *why* they bring about their own unhappiness and their self-destruction, *why* they are perverted and sick. And out of this has come the insight that human evil is largely (though not altogether) human weakness or ignorance, forgivable, understandable and also curable.

I find it sometimes amusing, sometimes saddening that so many scholars and scientists, so many philosophers and theologians, who talk about human values, of good and evil, proceed in complete disregard of the plain fact that professional psychotherapists every day, as a matter of course, change and improve human nature, help people to become more strong, virtuous, creative, kind, loving, altruistic, serene. These are only some of the consequences of improved self-knowledge and self-acceptance. There are many others as well that can come in greater or lesser degree (97, 144).

The subject is far too complex even to touch here. All I can do is draw a few conclusions for value theory.

1. Self-knowledge seems to be the major path of self-improvement, though not the only one.

2. Self-knowledge and self-improvement is very difficult for most people. It usually needs great courage and long struggle.

3. Though the help of a skilled professional therapist makes this process much easier, it is by no means the only way. Much that has been learned from therapy can be applied to education, to family life, and to the guidance of one's own life.

4. Only by such study of psychopathology and therapy can one learn a proper respect for and appreciation of the forces of fear, of regression, of defense, of safety. Respecting and understanding these forces makes it much more possible to help oneself and others to grow toward health. False optimism sooner or later means disillusionment, anger and hopelessness.

5. To sum up, we can never really understand human weakness without also understanding its healthy trends. Otherwise we make the mistake of pathologizing everything. But also we can never fully understand or help human strength without also understanding its weaknesses. Otherwise we fall into the errors of overoptimistic reliance on rationality alone.

If we wish to help humans to become more fully human, we must realize not only that they try to realize themselves but that they are also reluctant or afraid or unable to do so. Only by fully appreciating this dialectic between sickness and health can we help to tip the balance in favor of health.

Values, Growth, and Health

My thesis is, then: we can, in principle, have a descriptive, naturalistic science of human values; that the age-old mutually exclusive contrast between "what is" and "what ought to be" is in part a false one; that we can study the highest values or goals of human beings as we study the values of ants or horses or oak trees, or, for that matter, Martians. We can discover (rather than create or invent) which values men trend toward, yearn for, struggle for, as they improve themselves, and which values they lose as they get sick.

But we have seen this can be done fruitfully (at least at this time in history and with the limited techniques at our disposal) only if we differentiate healthy specimens from the rest of the population. We cannot average neurotic yearnings with healthy yearnings and come out with a usable product. (I can illustrate with one apothegm what would take me thousands of words to say. A biologist recently announced, "I have discovered the missing link between the anthropoid apes and civilized men. *It's us!*")

It appears to me that these values are uncovered as well as created or constructed, that they are intrinsic in the structure of human nature itself, that they are biologically and genetically based, as well as culturally developed, that I am describing them rather than inventing them or projecting them, or wishing for them ("the management assumes no responsibility for what is found").

I can put this in a more innocent way by proposing for the moment that I am studying the free choices or preferences of various kinds of human beings, sick or healthy, old or young, and under various circumstances. This of course we have a right to do just as we have the researcher's right to study the free choices of white rats or monkeys or neurotics. Much of the irrelevant and distracting arguing over values can be avoided by such a phrasing and it has the virtue also of stressing the scientific nature of the enterprise, removing it altogether from the realm of the a priori. (Anyway, my belief is that the concept "value" will soon be obsolete. It includes too much, means too many diverse things and has too long a history. Furthermore, these varied usages are not usually conscious. They therefore create confusion and I am tempted often to give up the word altogether. It is possible usually to use a more specific and therefore less confusing synonym.)

This more naturalistic and descriptive approach (more "scientific") also has the advantage of shifting the form of the questions from loaded questions, "ought" and "should" questions preladen with implicit, unexamined values, to the more usual empirical form of questions about When? Where? To whom?

How much? Under what conditions?, etc., i.e., to empirically testable questions.[16]

My next main set of hypotheses is that the so-called higher values, the eternal virtues, etc., etc., etc., are approximately what we find as the free choices, in the good situation, of those people whom we call relatively healthy (mature, evolved, self-fulfilled, individuated, etc.), when they are feeling at their best and strongest.

Or, to phrase this in a more descriptive way, such people, when they feel strong, if *really* free choice is possible, tend spontaneously to choose the true rather than the false, good rather than evil, beauty rather than ugliness, integration rather than dissociation, joy rather than sorrow, aliveness rather than deadness, uniqueness rather than stereotype, and so on for what I have already described as the B-values.

A subsidiary hypothesis is that tendencies to choose these same B-values can be seen weakly and dimly in all or most human beings, i.e., that these may be species-wide values which are seen most clearly and unmistakably, most strongly in healthy people, and that in these healthy people these higher values are least alloyed either by defensive (anxiety-instigated) values, or by what I shall refer to below as healthy-regressive, or "coasting,"[17] values.

Another very likely hypothesis is this: what healthy people choose is on the whole what is "good for them" in biological terms certainly, but perhaps also in other senses ("good for them" here means "conducing to their and others' self-actualization"). Furthermore, I suspect that what is good for the healthy persons (chosen by them) may very probably be good for the less healthy people, too, in the long run, and is what the sick ones would also choose if they could become better choosers. Another way of saying this is that healthy people are better choosers than unhealthy people. Or to turn this affirmation about in order to yield another set of implications, I propose that we explore the consequences of observing whatever our best specimens choose, and then assuming that these are the highest values for all mankind. That is, let us see what happens when we playfully treat them as biological assays, more sensitive versions of ourselves, more quickly conscious of what is good for us than we are ourselves. This is an assumption that, given enough time, we would eventually choose what they choose quickly. Or that we would sooner or later see the wisdom of their choices, and then make the same choices. Or that they perceive sharply and clearly where we perceive dimly.

I hypothesize also that the values *perceived* in the peak-experiences are roughly the same as the choice-values spoken of above. I do this to show that choice-values are only one kind of values.

Finally, I hypothesize that these same B-values which exist as preferences or motivations in our best specimens are to some degree the same as the values which describe the "good" work of art, or Nature in general, or the good external world. That is, I think that the B-values within the person are to some extent isomorphic with the same values perceived in the world, and that there is a mutually enhancing and strengthening dynamic relationship between these inner and outer values (108, 114).

To spell out only one implication here, these propositions affirm the existence of the highest values within human nature itself, to be discovered there. This is in sharp contradiction to the older and more customary beliefs that the highest values can come only from a supernatural God, or from some other source outside human nature itself.

Defining Human-ness

We must honestly accept and grapple with the real theoretical and logical difficulties that inhere in such theses. Each element in this definition itself needs definition, and, as we work with them, we find ourselves skirting on the edge of circularity. Some circularity we shall have to accept for the moment.

The "good human being" can be defined only against some criterion of humanness. Also, this criterion will almost certainly be a matter of degree, i.e., some people are more human than others, and "good" human beings, the "good specimens," are *very* human. This must be so because there are so many defining characteristics of humanness, each *sine qua non*, and yet not sufficient in itself, to determine humanness. Furthermore, many of these defining characters are themselves matters of degree and do not totally or sharply differentiate animals from men.

Here also we find the formulations of Robert Hartman (59) to be very useful. A good human being (or tiger or apple tree) is good to the extent that it fulfills or satisfies the concept "human being" (or tiger or apple tree).

From one point of view this is really a very simple solution and one that we use unconsciously all the time. The new mother asks the doctor, "Is my baby normal?" and he knows what she means without quibbling. The zoo-keeper buying tigers seeks for "good specimens," real tigery tigers, with all the tigerish traits well defined and fully developed. When I buy cebus monkeys for my lab I shall want good specimens also, good monkeyish monkeys, not peculiar or unusual ones, good *cebus* monkeys. If I ran across one without a prehensile tail, that would not be a good cebus monkey, even though that's fine in a tiger. And so also for the good apple tree, the good butterfly. The taxonomist chooses for his "type specimen" of a new species, the one to be deposited in a museum, to be the exemplar for the whole species, the best specimen he can get, the most mature, the most uncrippled, the most typical of all the qualities that define the species. The same principle holds in choosing a "good Renoir," or "the best Rubens," etc.

In exactly this same sense, we can pick the best specimens of the human species, people with all the parts proper to the species, with all the human capacities well developed and fully functioning, and without obvious illnesses of any kind, especially any that might harm the central, defining, *sine qua non* characteristics. These can be called "most fully human."

So far this is not too difficult a problem. But consider the additional difficulties presented by being a judge in a beauty contest, or buying a flock of sheep, or buying a dog for a pet. Here we confront, firstly, the questions of arbitrary cultural standards which can overwhelm and obliterate biopsychological determinants. Secondly, we confront the problem of domestication, that is to say, of an artificial and protected life. Here we must also remember that human beings may also be considered domesticated in some ways, especially our most protected ones, e.g., brain-injured people, young children, etc. Thirdly, we confront the need to differentiate the values of a dairy farmer from the values of cows.

Since man's instinctoid tendencies, such as they are, are far weaker than cultural forces, it will always be a difficult task to tease out man's psychobiological values. Difficult or not, it is possible in principle. And also it is quite necessary, even crucial (97, Chapter 7).

Our big research problem is then "to choose the healthy chooser." For *practical* purposes, this can be done well enough right now, as physicians can now choose physically healthy organisms. The great difficulties here are *theoretical* ones, problems of the definition and conceptualizations of health.

Growth Values, Defensive-Values (Unhealthy Regression, and Healthy-regression Values ("Coasting" Values)

Under really free choice we find mature or healthier people valuing not only truth, goodness and beauty but also the regressive, survival and/or homeostatic values of peace and quiet, of sleep and rest, of surrender, of dependency and safety, or protection from reality and relief from it, of slipping back from Shakespeare to detective stories, of retiring into fantasy, even of wishing for death (peace), etc. We may call them crudely the growth values and the healthy-regressive, or "coasting," values, and point out further that the more mature, strong and healthy the person, the more he seeks growth values and the less he seeks and needs "coasting" values; but he still needs both. These two sets of values stand always in a dialectical relation to each other, yielding up the dynamic equilibrium that is overt behavior.

It must be remembered that the basic motivations supply ready-made an hierarchy of values which are related to each other as higher needs and lower needs, stronger and weaker, more vital and more dispensable.

These needs are arranged in an integrated hierarchy rather than dichotomously, that is, they rest one upon another. The higher need for actualization of special talents, let us say, rests upon the continued gratification of, let us say, the safety needs, which do not disappear even though in a non-active state. (By inactive, I mean the condition of hunger after a good meal.)

This means that the process of regression to lower needs remains always as a possibility, and in this context must be seen *not* only as pathological or sick, but as absolutely necessary to the integrity of the whole organism, and as prerequisite to the existence and functioning of the "higher needs." Safety is a *sine qua non* precondition for love, which is a precondition for self-actualization.

Therefore these healthily regressive value-choices must be considered as "normal," natural, healthy, instinctoid, etc., as the so-called "higher values." It is clear also that they stand in a dialectic or dynamic relation to each other (or, as I prefer to say, they are hierarchically-integrated rather than dichotomous). And finally we must deal with the clear, descriptive fact that lower needs and values are prepotent over higher needs and values most of the time for most of the population, i.e., that they exert a strong regressive pull. It is only in the healthiest, most mature, most evolved individuals that higher values are chosen and preferred consistently more often (and that only under good or fairly good life circumstances). And this probably is true largely because of the solid basis of gratified lower needs which, because of their dormancy and inactivity through gratification, do not exert a regressive pull backward. (And it is as obviously true that this assumption of need gratification assumes a pretty good world.)

An old-fashioned way of summarizing this is to say that man's higher nature rests upon man's lower nature, needing it as a foundation and collapsing without this foundation. That is, man's higher nature is inconceivable without a satisfied lower nature as a base. The best way to develop this higher nature is to fulfill and gratify the lower nature first. Furthermore, man's higher nature rests also on the existence of a good or fairly good environment, present and previous.

The implication here is that man's higher nature, ideals, and aspirations, and abilities rest not upon instinctual renunciation, but rather upon instinctual gratification. (Of course the "basic needs" I've been talking about are not the same as the "instincts" of the classical Freudians.) Even so, the way in which I have phrased it points to the necessity of a re-examination of Freud's theory of instincts. This is long overdue. On the other hand, this phrasing has some isomorphism with Freud's metaphorical dichotomy of life and death instincts. Perhaps we can use his basic metaphor while modifying the concrete phrasing. This dialectic between progression and regression, between higher and lower, is now being phrased in another way by the existentialists. I don't see any great difference between these phrasings except that I try to make mine closer to the empirical and clinical materials, more confirmable or disconfirmable.

The Existential Human Dilemma

Even our best people are not exempted from the basic human predicament, of being simultaneously merely-creaturely and godlike, strong and weak, limited and unlimited, merely-animal and animal-transcending, adult and child, fearful and courageous, progressing and regressing, yearning for perfection and yet afraid of it, being a worm and also a hero. This is what the existentialists keep trying to tell us. I feel we must agree with them on the basis of the evidence we have available that this dilemma and its dialectic are basic to any ultimate system of psychodynamics and psychotherapy. Furthermore, I consider it basic to any naturalistic theory of values.

It is extremely important, however, even crucial, to give up our 3,000-year-old habit of dichotomizing, splitting and separating in the style of Aristotelian logic, ("A and Not-A are wholly different from each other, and are mutually exclusive. Take your choice—one *or* the other. But you can't have both.") Difficult though it may be, we must learn to think holistically rather than atomistically. All these "opposites" are in fact hierarchically-integrated, especially in healthier people, and one of the proper goals of therapy is to move from dichotomizing and splitting toward integration of seemingly irreconcilable opposites. Our godlike qualities rest upon and need our animal qualities. Our adulthood should not be only a renunciation of childhood, but an inclusion of its good values and a building upon it. Higher values are hierarchically-integrated with lower values. Ultimately, dichotomizing pathologizes, and pathology dichotomizes. (Compare with Goldstein's (55) powerful concept of isolation.)

Intrinsic Values as Possibilities

Values are partly discovered by us within ourselves as I have said. But they are also partly created or chosen by the person himself. Discovery is not the only way of deriving the values by which we shall live. It is rare that self-search discovers something strictly univocal, a finger pointing in one direction only, a need satisfiable in only one way. Almost all needs, capacities and talents can be satisfied in a variety of ways. Though this variety is limited, still it *is* a variety. The born athlete has many sports to choose from. The love-need can be satisfied by any one of many people and in a variety of ways. The talented musician can be almost as happy with a flute as with a clarinet. A great intellectual could be equally happy as a biologist or as a chemist or psychologist. For any man of good will, there are a great variety of causes, or duties, to dedicate himself to with equal satisfaction. One might say that this inner structure of human nature is cartilaginous rather than bony; or that it can be trained and guided like a hedge or even espaliered like a fruit tree.

The problems of choice and renunciation still remain even though a good tester or therapist should be able soon to see in a general way what the talents and capacities and needs of the person are and be able, e.g., to give him pretty decent vocational guidance.

Furthermore, as the growing person dimly sees the range of fates from among which he can choose, in accordance with opportunity, with cultural praise or blame, etc., and as he gradually commits himself (chooses? is chosen?), let us say, to becoming a physician, the problems of self-making and self-creating soon emerge. Discipline, hard work, postponement of pleasure, forcing himself, moulding and training himself, all become necessary even for the "born physician." No matter how much he loves his work, there are still chores that must be swallowed for the sake of the whole.

Or to put it another way, self-actualization via being a physician means being a good physician, not a poor one. This ideal certainly is partly created by him, partly given to him by the culture and partly discovered within himself. What he thinks a good physician ought to be is as determinative as his own talents, capacities and needs.

Can Uncovering Therapies Help In Search for Values

Hartmann (61, pp. 51, 60, 85) denies that moral imperatives can legitimately be derived from psychoanalytic findings (but see also p. 92) .[18] What does "derived" mean here? What I am claiming is that psychoanalysis and other uncovering therapies simply *reveal* or expose an inner, more biological, more instinctoid core of human nature. Part of this core are certain preferences and yearnings that may be considered to be intrinsic, biologically based values, even though weak ones. All the basic needs fall into this category and so do all the inborn capacities and talents of the individual. I do not say these are "oughts" or "moral imperatives," at least not in the old, external sense. I say only that they are intrinsic to human nature and that furthermore their denial and frustration make for psychopathology and therefore for evil, for though not synonymous, pathology and evil certainly overlap.

Similarly Redlich (109 p. 88), says, "If the quest for therapy becomes a quest for ideology, it is bound to be disappointed, as Wheelis clearly stated, because psychoanalysis cannot provide an ideology." Of course, this is true, if we take the word "ideology" literally.

And yet again something very important is overlooked thereby. Though these uncovering therapies do not *provide* an ideology, they certainly help to *uncover* and lay bare at least the *anlagen* or rudiments of intrinsic values.

That is, the uncovering, depth therapist can help a patient to discover what deepest, most intrinsic values he (the patient) is pursuing obscurely, yearning for, needing. Therefore, I maintain that the right sort of therapy *is* relevant to the search for values rather than irrelevant as Wheelis (174) claims. Indeed, I think it possible that we may soon even *define* therapy as a search for values, because ultimately the search for identity, is, in essence, the search for one's own intrinsic, authentic values. Especially is this clear when we remember that improved self-knowledge (and clarity of one's values) is also coincident with improved knowledge of others and of reality in general (and clarity of *their* values).

Finally, I consider it to be possible that the current over-stress on the (supposedly) great gap between self-knowledge and ethical action (and value commitment) may itself be a symptom of the specifically *obsessional* hiatus between thought and action which is not so general for other types of character (but see 32). This can probably also be generalized to the age-old dichotomy among the philosophers between "is" and "ought," between fact and norm. My observation of healthier people, of people in peak experiences, and of people who manage to integrate their good obsessional qualities with the good hysterical qualities, is that in general there is no such *unbridgeable* chasm or hiatus; that in them, clear knowledge generally flows right over into spontaneous action or ethical commitment. That is, when they *know* what is the right thing to do, they do it. What is left over in healthier people of this gap between knowledge and action? Only what is inherent in reality and in existence, only real problems rather than pseudo-problems.

To the extent that this suspicion is correct, to that extent are the depth, uncovering therapies validated not only as sickness-removers but also as legitimate value-uncovering techniques.

Health as Transcendence of Environment

My purpose is to save one point that may get lost in the current wave of discussion of mental health. The danger that I see is the resurgence, in new and more sophisticated forms, of the old identification of psychological health with adjustment, adjustment to reality, adjustment to society, adjustment to other people. That is, the authentic or healthy person may be defined not in his own right, not in his autonomy, not by his own intra-psychic and non-environmental laws, not as *different* from the environment, independent of it or opposed to it, but rather in environment-centered terms, e.g., of ability to master the environment, to be capable, adequate, effective, competent in relation to *it*, to do a good job, to perceive *it* well, to be in good relations to *it*, to be successful in *its* terms. To say it in another way, the job-analysis, the requirements of the task, should not be the major criterion of worth or health of the individual. There is not only an orientation to the outer but also to the inner. An extra-psychic centering point cannot be used for the theoretical task of defining the healthy psyche. We must not fall into the trap of defining the good organism in terms of what he is "good for" as if he were an instrument rather than something in himself, as if he were only a means to some extrinsic purpose. (As I understand Marxist psychology, it also is a very blunt and unmistakable expression of the view that the psyche is a mirror to reality.)

I am thinking especially of Robert White's recent paper in the *Psychological Review*, "Motivation Reconsidered," (177) and Robert Woodworth's book, *Dynamics of Behavior* (184). I have chosen these because they are excellent jobs, highly sophisticated, and because they have carried motivation theory forward in a huge leap. As far as they go, I agree with them. But I feel they don't go far enough. They contain in a hidden form the danger that I have referred to, that, although mastery, effectance and competence may be active rather than passive styles of adjustment to reality, they are *still* variations of adjustment theory. I feel we must leap beyond these statements, admirable though they may be, to the clear recognition of transcendence[19] of the environment, independence of it, ability to stand against it, to fight it, to neglect it, or to turn one's back on it, to refuse it or adapt to it. (I pass by the temptation to discuss the masculine, Western and American character of these terms. Would a woman, a Hindu, or even a Frenchman think primarily in terms of mastery or competence?) For a theory of mental health, extra-psychic success is not enough; we must also include intra-psychic health.

Another example which I wouldn't take seriously were it not that so many others *do* take it seriously, is the Harry Stack Sullivan type of effort to define a Self simply in terms of what other people think of him, an extreme cultural relativity in which a healthy individuality gets lost altogether. Not that this isn't true for the immature personality. It is. But we are talking about the healthy fully-grown person. And *he* certainly is characterized by his transcendence of other people's opinions.

To substantiate my conviction that we must save the differentiation between self and not-self in order to understand the fully matured person (authentic, self-actualizing, individuated, productive, healthy), I call attention to the following considerations, very briefly presented, of course.

1. First I mention some data I presented in a 1951 paper called "Resistance to Acculturation"(96). I reported my healthy subjects to be superficially accepting of conventions, but privately to be casual, perfunctory and detached about them. That is, they could take them or leave them. In practically all of them, I found a rather calm, good-humored rejection of the stupidities and imperfections of the culture with greater or lesser effort at improving it. They definitely showed an ability to fight it vigorously when they thought it necessary. To quote from this paper: "The mixture of varying proportions of affection or approval, and hostility and criticism indicated that they select from American culture what is good in it by their lights and reject what they think bad in it. In a word, they weigh it, and judge it (by their own inner criteria) and then make their own decisions."

They also showed a surprising amount of detachment from people in general and a strong liking for privacy, even a need for it (97).

"For these and other reasons they may be called autonomous, i.e., ruled by the laws of their own character rather than by the rules of society (insofar as these are different). It is in this sense that they are not only or merely Americans but also members at large of the human species. I then hypothesized that" these people should have less 'national character,' and that they should be more like each other across cultural lines than they are like the less-developed members of their own culture."[20]

The point I wish to stress here is the detachment, the independence, the self-governing character of these people, the tendency to look within for the guiding values and rules to live by.

2. Furthermore, only by such a differentiation can we leave a theoretical place for meditation, contemplation and for all other forms of going into the Self, of turning away from the outer world in order to listen to the inner voices. This includes all the processes of all the insight therapies, in which turning

away from the world is a *sine qua non,* in which the path to health is via turning into the fantasies, the primary processes, that is, via the recovery of the intrapsychic in general. The psychoanalytic couch is outside the culture to the extent that this is possible. (In any fuller discussion, I would certainly argue the case for an enjoyment of consciousness itself and for experience-values; 28, 124.)

3. The recent interest in health, creativeness, art, play and love has taught us much, I think, about *general* psychology. From among the various consequences of these explorations, I would pick out one to emphasize for our present purposes, and that is the change in attitude toward the depths of human nature, the unconscious, the primary processes, the archaic, the mythological and the poetic. Because the roots of ill health were found first in the unconscious, it has been our tendency to think of the unconscious as bad, evil, crazy, dirty or dangerous, and to think of the primary processes as *distorting* the truth. But now that we have found these depths to be also the source of creativeness, of art, of love, of humor and play, and even of certain kinds of truth and knowledge, we can begin to speak of a healthy unconscious, of healthy regressions. And especially can we begin to value primary process cognition and archaic or mythological thinking instead of considering them to be pathological. We can now go into primary process cognitions for certain kinds of knowledge, not only about the self but also about the world, to which secondary processes are blind. These primary processes are part of normal or healthy human nature and must be included in any comprehensive theory of healthy human nature (84, 100).

If you agree with this, then you must wrestle with the fact that they are intrapsychic and have their own autochthonous laws and rules, that they are not *primarily* adapted to external reality or shaped by it or equipped to cope with it. More superficial layers of the personality differentiate out to take care of this job. To identify the whole psyche with these tools for coping with the environment is to lose something which we no longer dare to lose. Adequacy, adjustment, adaptation, competence, mastery, coping, these are all environment-oriented words and are therefore inadequate to describe the *whole* psyche, part of which has nothing to do with the environment.

4. The distinction between the coping aspect of behavior and the expressive aspect is also important here. On various grounds I have challenged the axiom that all behavior is motivated. Here I would stress the fact that expressive behavior is either unmotivated or, anyway, less motivated than coping behavior (depending on what you mean by 'motivated'). In their purer form, expressive behaviors have little to do with environment, and do not have the purpose of

changing it or adapting to it. The words adaptation, adequacy, competence or mastery do not apply to expressive behaviors but only to coping behaviors. A reality-centered theory of full human nature cannot manage or incorporate expression, unless with great difficulty. The natural and easy centering-point from which to understand expressive behavior is intra-psychic (97, Chapter 11).

5. Being focused on a task produces organization for efficiency both within the organism and in the environment. What is irrelevant is pushed aside and not noticed. The various relevant capacities and information arrange themselves under the hegemony of a goal, a purpose, which means that importance becomes defined in terms of that which help to solve the problem; i.e., in terms of usefulness. What doesn't help to solve the problem becomes unimportant. Selection becomes necessary. So does abstraction, which means also blindness to some things, inattention, exclusion.

But we have learned that motivated perception, task-orientation, cognition in terms of usefulness, which are all involved in effectance and in competence (which White defines as "an organism's capacity to interact effectively with its environment") leaves out something, and therefore is a partial blindness. For cognition to be complete, I have shown that it must be detached, disinterested, desireless, unmotivated. Only thus are we able to perceive the object in its own nature with its own objective, intrinsic characteristics rather than abstracting it down to "what is useful," "what is threatening,"etc.

To the extent that we try to master the environment or be effective with it, to that extent do we cut the possibility of full, objective, detached, non-interfering cognition. Only if we let it be, can we perceive fully. Again, to cite psychotherapeutic experience, the more eager we are to make a diagnosis and a plan of action, the *less* helpful do we become. The more eager we are to cure, the longer it takes. Every psychiatric researcher has to learn not to *try* to cure, *not* to be impatient. In this and in many other situations, to give in is to overcome, to be humble is to succeed. The Taoists and Zen Buddhists taking this path were able a thousand years ago to see what we psychologists are only beginning to be aware of.

But most important is my preliminary finding that this kind of cognition of the Being (B-cognition) of the world is found more often in healthy people and may even turn out to be one of the defining characteristics of health. I have also found it in the peak-experiences (transient self-actualizing). This implies that even with regard to healthy relations with the environment the words mastery, competence, effectiveness suggest far more active purposefulness than is wise for a concept of health.

As a single example of the consequence of this change in attitude toward unconscious processes, it can be hypothesized that sensory deprivation instead of only frightening should for healthy people also be pleasing. That is, since cutting off the outer world seems to permit the inner world to come to consciousness, and since the inner world is more accepted and enjoyed by healthier people, then they should be more likely to enjoy sensory deprivation.

Summary

What these considerations can teach us about the theory of health is:

1. We cannot obliterate the autonomous self or pure psyche. It must not be treated as *only* an adaptational instrument.

2. Even when we deal with our relations with environment, we must make a theoretical place for a receptive relation to the environment as well as a masterful one.

3. Psychology is in part a branch of biology, in part a branch of sociology. But it is not *only* that. It has its own unique jurisdiction as well, that portion of the psyche which is *not* a reflection of the outer world or a molding to it. There could be such a thing as a psychological psychology.

Part VI

Future Tasks

Some Basic Propositions of a Growth and Self-Actualization Psychology

When the philosophy of man (his nature, his goals, his potentialities, his fulfillment) changes, then everything changes, not only the philosophy of politics, of economics, of ethics and values, of interpersonal relations and of history itself, but also the philosophy of education, the theory of how to help men become what they can and deeply need to become.

We are now in the middle of such a change in the conception of man's capacities, potentialities and goals. A new vision is emerging of the possibilities of man and of his destiny, and its implications are many, not only for our conceptions of education, but also for science, politics, literature, economics, religion, and even our conceptions of the non-human world.

I think it is now possible to begin to delineate this view of human nature as a total, single, comprehensive system of psychology even though much of it has arisen as a reaction *against* the limitations (as philosophies of human nature) of the two most comprehensive psychologies now available—behaviorism (or associationism) and classical, Freudian psychoanalysis. Finding a single label for it is still a difficult task, perhaps a premature one. In the past I have called it the "holistic-dynamic" psychology to express my conviction about its major roots. Some have called it "organismic" following Goldstein. Sutich and others are calling it the Self-psychology or Humanistic psychology. We shall see. My own guess is that, in a few decades, if it remains suitably eclectic and comprehensive, it will be called simply "psychology."

I think I can be of most service by speaking primarily for myself and out of my own work rather than as an "official" delegate of this large group of thinkers, even though I am sure that the areas of agreement among them are very large. A selection of works of this "third force" is listed in the bibliography. Because of the limited space I have, I will present here only some of the major propositions of this point of view, especially those of importance to the educator. I should warn you that at many points I am way out ahead of the data. Some of these propositions are more based on private conviction than on publicly demonstrated facts. However, they are all in principle confirmable or disconfirmable.

1. We have, each one of us, an essential inner nature which is instinctoid, intrinsic, given, "natural," i.e., with an appreciable hereditary determinant, and which tends strongly to persist (97, Chapter 7).

It makes sense to speak here of the hereditary, constitutional and very early acquired roots of the *individual* self, even though this biological determination of self is only partial, and far too complex to describe simply. In any case, this is "raw material" rather than finished product, to be reacted to by the person, by his significant others, by his environment, etc.

I include in this essential inner nature instinctoid basic needs, capacities, talents, anatomical equipment, physiological or temperamental balances, prenatal and natal injuries, and traumata to the neonate. This inner core shows itself as natural inclinations, propensities or inner bent. Whether defense and coping mechanisms, "style of life," and other characterological traits, all shaped in the first few years of life, should be included is still a matter for discussion. This raw material very quickly starts growing into a self as it meets the world outside and begins to have transaction with it.

2. These are potentialities, not final actualizations. Therefore they have a life history and must be seen developmentally. They are actualized, shaped or stifled mostly (but not altogether) by extra-psychic determinants (culture, family, environment, learning, etc.). Very early in life these goalless urges and tendencies become attached to objects ("sentiments") by canalization (122) but also by arbitrarily learned associations.

3. This inner core, even though it is biologically based and "instinctoid," is weak in certain senses rather than strong. It is easily overcome, suppressed or repressed. It may even be killed off permanently. Humans no longer have instincts in the animal sense, powerful, unmistakable inner voices which tell them unequivocally what to do, when, where, how and with whom. All that we have left are instinct-remnants. And furthermore, these are weak, subtle and delicate, very easily drowned out by learning, by cultural expectations, by fear, by disapproval, etc. They are *hard* to know, rather than easy. Authentic selfhood can be defined in part as being able to hear these impulse-voices within oneself, i.e., to know what one really wants or doesn't want, what one is fit for and what one is *not* fit for, etc. It appears that there are wide individual differences in the strength of these impulse-voices.

4. Each person's inner nature has some characteristics which all other selves have (species-wide) and some which are unique to the person (idiosyncratic).

The need for love characterizes every human being that is born (although it can disappear later under certain circumstances). Musical genius however is given to very few, and these differ markedly from each other in style, e.g., Mozart and Debussy.

5. It is possible to study this inner nature scientifically and objectively (that is, with the right kind of "science") and to discover what it is like (discover—not invent or construct). It is also possible to do this subjectively, by inner search and by psychotherapy, and the two enterprises supplement and support each other.

6. Many aspects of this inner, deeper nature are either (a) actively repressed, as Freud has described, because they are feared or disapproved of or are ego-alien, or (b) "forgotten" (neglected, unused, overlooked, unverbalized or suppressed), as Schachtel has described. Much of the inner, deeper nature is therefore unconscious. This can be true not only for impulses (drives, instincts, needs) as Freud has stressed, but also for capacities, emotions, judgments, attitudes, definitions, perceptions, etc. Active repression takes effort and uses up energy. There are many specific techniques of maintaining active unconsciousness, such as denial, projection, reaction-formation, etc. However, repression does not kill what is repressed. The repressed remains as one active determinant of thought and behavior.

Both active and passive repressions seem to begin early in life, mostly as a response to parental and cultural disapprovals.

However, there is some clinical evidence that repression may arise also from intra-psychic, extra-cultural sources in the young child, or at puberty, i.e., out of fear of being overwhelmed by its own impulses, of becoming disintegrated, of "falling apart," exploding, etc. It is theoretically possible that the child may spontaneously form attitudes of fear and disapproval toward its own impulses and may then defend himself against them in various ways. Society need not be the only repressing force, if this is true. There may also be intra-psychic re-pressing and controlling forces. These we may call "intrinsic counter-cathexes."

It is best to distinguish unconscious drives and needs from unconscious ways of cognizing because the latter are often easier to bring to consciousness and therefore to modify. Primary process cognition (Freud) or archaic thinking (Jung) is more recoverable by, e.g., creative art education, dance education, and other non-verbal educational techniques.

7. Even though "weak," this inner nature rarely disappears or dies, in the usual person, in the U. S. (such disappearance or dying is possible early in the life history, however). It persists underground, unconsciously, even though denied and repressed. Like the voice of the intellect (which is part of it), it speaks softly but it *will* be heard, even if in a distorted form. That is, it has a dynamic force of its own, pressing always for open, uninhibited expression. Effort must be used in its suppression or repression from which fatigue can result. This force is one main aspect of the "will to health," the urge to grow, the pressure to self-actualization, the quest for one's identity. It is this that makes psychotherapy, education and self-improvement possible in principle.

8. However, this inner core, or self, grows into adulthood only partly by (objective or subjective) discovery, uncovering and acceptance of what is "there" beforehand. Partly it is also a creation of the person himself. Life is a continual series of choices for the individual in which a main determinant of choice is the person as he already is (including his goals for himself, his courage or fear, his feeling of responsibility, his ego-strength or "will power," etc.). We can no longer think of the person as "fully determined" where this phrase implies "determined only by forces external to the person." The person, insofar as he *is* a real person, is his own main determinant. Every person is, in part, "his own project" and makes himself.

9. If this essential core (inner nature) of the person is frustrated, denied or suppressed, sickness results, sometimes in obvious forms, sometimes in subtle and devious forms, sometimes immediately, sometimes later. These psychological illnesses include many more than those listed by the American Psychiatric Association. For instance, the character disorders and disturbances are now seen as far more important for the fate of the world than the classical neuroses or even the psychoses. From this new point of view, new kinds of illness are most dangerous, e.g., "the diminished or stunted person," i.e., the loss of any of the defining characteristics of humanness, or personhood, the failure to grow to one's potential, valuelessness, etc.

That is, general-illness of the personality is seen as any falling short of growth, or of self-actualization, or of full-humanness. And the main source of illness (although not the only one) is seen as frustrations (of the basic needs, of the B-values, of idiosyncratic potentials, of expression of the self, and of the tendency of the person to grow in his own style and at his own pace) especially in the early years of life. That is, frustration of the basic needs is not the only source of illness or of human diminution.

10. This inner nature, as much as we know of it so far, is definitely not "evil," but is either what we adults in our culture call "good," or else it is neutral. The most accurate way to express this is to say that it is "prior to good and evil." There is little question about this if we speak of the inner nature of the infant and child. The statement is much more complex if we speak of the "infant" as he still exists in the adult. And it gets still more complex if the individual is seen from the point of view of B-psychology rather than D-psychology.

This conclusion is supported by all the truth-revealing and uncovering techniques that have anything to do with human nature: psychotherapy, objective science, subjective science, education and art. For instance, in the long run, uncovering therapy lessens hostility, fear, greed, etc., and increases love, courage, creativeness, kindness, altruism, etc., leading us to the conclusion that the latter are "deeper," more natural, and more basic than the former, i.e., that what we call "bad" behavior is lessened or removed by uncovering, while what we call "good" behavior is strengthened and fostered by uncovering.

11. We must differentiate the Freudian type of superego from intrinsic conscience and intrinsic guilt. The former is in principle a taking into the self of the disapprovals and approvals of persons other than the person himself, fathers, mothers, teachers, etc. Guilt then is recognition of disapproval by others.

Intrinsic guilt is the consequence of betrayal of one's own inner nature or self, a turning off the path to self-actualization, and is essentially justified self-disapproval. It is therefore not as culturally relative as is Freudian guilt. It is "true" or "deserved" or "right and just" or "correct" because it is a discrepancy from something profoundly real within the person rather than from accidental, arbitrary or purely relative localisms. Seen in this way it is good, even *necessary*, for a person's development to have intrinsic guilt when he deserves to. It is not just a symptom to be avoided at any cost but is rather an inner guide for growth toward actualization of the real self, and of its potentialities.

12. "Evil" behavior has mostly referred to unwarranted hostility, cruelty, destructiveness, "mean" aggressiveness. This we do not know enough about. To the degree that this quality of hostility is instinctoid, mankind has one kind of future. To the degree that it is reactive (a response to bad treatment), mankind has a very different kind of future. My opinion is that the weight of the evidence so far indicates that indiscriminately *destructive* hostility is reactive, because uncovering therapy reduces it, and changes its quality into "healthy"

self-affirmation, forcefulness, selective hostility, self-defense, righteous indignation, etc. In any case, the *ability* to be aggressive and angry is found in all self-actualizing people, who are able to let it flow forth freely when the external situation "calls for" it.

The situation in children is far more complex. At the very least, we know that the healthy child is also able to be justifiably angry, self-protecting and self-affirming, i.e., reactive aggression. Presumably, then, a child should learn not only how to control his anger, but also how and when to express it.

Behavior that our culture calls evil can also come from ignorance and from childish misinterpretations and beliefs (whether in the child or in the repressed or "forgotten" child-in-the-adult). For instance, sibling rivalry is traceable to the child's wish for the exclusive love of his parents. Only as he matures is he in principle capable of learning that his mother's love for a sibling is compatible with her continued love for him. Thus out of a childish version of love, not in itself reprehensible, can come unloving behavior.

The commonly seen hatred or resentment of or jealousy of goodness, truth, beauty, health or intelligence, ("counter-values") is largely (though not altogether) determined by threat of loss of self-esteem, as the liar is threatened by the honest man, the homely girl by the beautiful girl, or the coward by the hero. Every superior person confronts us with our own shortcomings.

Still deeper than this, however, is the ultimate existential question of the fairness and justice of fate. The person with a disease may be jealous of the healthy man who is no more deserving than he.

Evil behaviors seem to most psychologists to be reactive as in these examples, rather than instinctive. This implies that though "bad" behavior is very deeply rooted in human nature and can never be abolished altogether, it may yet be expected to lessen as the personality matures and as the society improves.

13. Many people still think of "the unconscious," of regression, and of primary process cognition as necessarily unhealthy, or dangerous or bad. Psychotherapeutic experience is slowly teaching us otherwise. Our depths can also be good, or beautiful or desirable. This is also becoming clear from the general findings from investigations of the sources of love, creativeness, play, humor, art, etc. Their roots are deep in the inner, deeper self, i.e., in the unconscious. To recover them and to be able to enjoy and use them we must be able to "regress."

14. No psychological health is possible unless this essential core of the person is fundamentally accepted, loved and respected by others and by himself

(the converse is not necessarily true, i.e., that if the core is respected, etc., then psychological health must result, since other prerequisite conditions must also be satisfied).

The psychological health of the chronologically immature is called healthy growth. The psychological health of the adult is called variously, self-fulfillment, emotional maturity, individuation, productiveness, self-actualization, authenticity, full-humanness, etc.

Healthy growth is conceptually subordinate, for it is usually defined now as "growth toward self-actualization," etc. Some psychologists speak simply in terms of one overarching goal or end, or tendency of human development, considering all immature growth phenomena to be only steps along the path to self-actualization (Goldstein, Rogers).

Self-actualization is defined in various ways but a solid core of agreement is perceptible. All definitions accept or imply, (a) acceptance and expression of the inner core or self, i.e., actualization of these latent capacities, and potentialities, "full functioning," availability of the human and personal essence. (b) They all imply minimal presence of ill health, neurosis, psychosis, of loss or diminution of the basic human and personal capacities.

15. For all these reasons, it is at this time best to bring out and encourage, or at the very least, to recognize this inner nature, rather than to suppress or repress it. Pure spontaneity consists of free, uninhibited, uncontrolled, trusting, unpremeditated expression of the self, i.e., of the psychic forces, with minimal interference by consciousness. Control, will, caution, self-criticism, measure, deliberateness are the brakes upon this expression made intrinsically necessary by the laws of the social and natural worlds outside the psychic world, and secondarily, made necessary by fear of the psyche itself (intrinsic counter-cathexis). Speaking in a very broad way, controls upon the psyche which come from *fear of the psyche ate* largely neurotic or *psychotic*, or not intrinsically or theoretically necessary. (The healthy psyche is not terrible or horrible and therefore doesn't have to be feared, as it has been for thousands of years. Of course, the *unhealthy* psyche is another story.) This kind of control is usually lessened by psychological health, by deep psychotherapy, or by any *deeper* self-knowledge and self-acceptance. There are also, however, controls upon the psyche which do not come out of fear, but out of the necessities for keeping it integrated, organized and unified (intrinsic counter-cathexes). And there are also "controls," probably in another sense, which are necessary as capacities are actualized, and as higher forms of expression are sought for, e.g., acquisition of skills through hard work by the artist, the intellectual, the athlete. But these

controls are eventually transcended and become aspects of spontaneity, as they become self.

The balance between spontaneity and control varies, then, as the health of the psyche and the health of the world vary. Pure spontaneity is not long possible because we live in a world which runs by its own, non-psychic laws. It *is* possible in dreams, fantasies, love, imagination, sex, the first stages of creativity, artistic work, intellectual play, free association, etc. Pure control is not permanently possible, for then the psyche dies. Education must be directed then *both* toward cultivation of controls and cultivation of spontaneity and expression. In our culture and at this point in history, it is necessary to redress the balance in favor of spontaneity, the ability to be expressive, passive, unwilled, trusting in processes other than will and control, unpremeditated, creative, etc. But it must be recognized that there have been and will be other cultures and other areas in which the balance was or will be in the other direction.

16. In the normal development of the normal child, it is now known that, *most* of the time, if he is given a really free choice, he will choose what is good for his growth. This he does because it tastes good, feels good, gives pleasure or *delight*. This implies that *he* "knows" better than anyone else what is good for him. A permissive regime means not that adults gratify his needs directly but make it possible for *him* to gratify his needs, and make his own choices, i.e., let him *be*. It is necessary in order for children to grow well that adults have enough trust in them and in the natural processes of growth, i.e., not interfere too much, not *make* them grow, or force them into predetermined designs, but rather *let* them grow and *help* them grow in a Taoistic rather than an authoritarian way.

17. Coordinate with this "acceptance" of the self, of fate, of one's call, is the conclusion that the main path to health and self-fulfillment for the masses is via basic need gratification rather than via frustration. This contrasts with the suppressive regime, the mistrust, the control, the policing that is necessarily implied by the belief in basic, instinctive evil in the human depths. Intrauterine life is completely gratifying and non-frustrating and it is now generally accepted that the first year or so of life had better also be primarily gratifying and non-frustrating. Asceticism, self-denial, deliberate rejection of the demands of the organism, at least in the West, tend to produce a diminished, stunted or crippled organism, and even in the East, bring self-actualization to only a very few, exceptionally strong individuals.

18. But we know also that the *complete absence* of frustration is dangerous. To be strong, a person must acquire frustration-tolerance, the ability to perceive physical reality as essentially indifferent to human wishes, the ability to love others and to enjoy their need-gratification as well as one's own (not to use other people only as means). The child with a good basis of safety, love and respect-need-gratification, is able to profit from nicely graded frustrations and become stronger thereby. If they are more than he can bear, if they overwhelm him, we call them traumatic, and consider them dangerous rather than profitable.

It is via the frustrating unyieldingness of physical reality and of animals and of other people that we learn about *their* nature, and thereby learn to differentiate wishes from facts (which things wishing makes come true, and which things proceed in complete disregard of our wishes), and are thereby enabled to live in the world and adapt to it as necessary.

We learn also about our own strengths and limits and extend them by overcoming difficulties, by straining ourselves to the utmost, by meeting challenge and hardship, even by failing. There can be great enjoyment in a great struggle and this can displace fear.

Overprotection implies that the child's needs are gratified *for* him by his parents, without effort of his own. This tends to infantilize him, to prevent development of his own strength, will and self-assertion. In one of its forms it may teach him to use other people rather than to respect them. In another form it implies a lack of trust and respect for the child's own powers and choices, i.e., it is essentially condescending and insulting, and can help to make a child feel worthless.

19. To make growth and self-actualization possible, it is necessary to understand that capacities, organs and organ systems press to function and express themselves and to be used and exercised, and that such use is satisfying, and disuse irritating. The muscular person likes to use his muscles, indeed, *has* to use them in order to "feel good" and to achieve the subjective feeling of harmonious, successful, uninhibited functioning (spontaneity) which is so important an aspect of good growth and psychological health. So also for intelligence, for the uterus, the eyes, the capacity to love. Capacities clamor to be used, and cease their clamor only when they *are* well used. That is, capacities are also needs. Not only is it fun to use our capacities, but it is also necessary for growth. The unused skill or capacity or organ can become a disease center or else atrophy or disappear, thus diminishing the person.

20. The psychologist proceeds on the assumption that for his purposes there are two kinds of worlds, two kinds of reality, the natural world and the psychic world, the world of unyielding facts and the world of wishes, hopes, fears, emotions, the world which runs by non-psychic rules and the world which runs by psychic laws. This differentiation is not very clear except at its extremes, where there is no doubt that delusions, dreams and free associations are lawful and yet utterly different from the lawfulness of logic and from the lawfulness of the world which would remain if the human species died out. This assumption does not deny that these worlds are related and may even fuse.

I may say that this assumption is acted upon by *many* or *most* pychologists, even though they are perfectly willing to admit that it is an insoluble philosophical problem. Any therapist *must* assume it or give up his functioning. This is typical of the way in which psychologists bypass philosophical difficulties and act "as if" certain assumptions were true even though unprovable, e.g., the universal assumption of "responsibility," "will power," etc. One aspect of health is the ability to live in both of these worlds.

21. Immaturity can be contrasted with maturity from the motivational point of view, as the process of gratifying the deficiency-needs in their proper order. Maturity, or self-actualization, from this point of view, means to transcend the deficiency-needs. This state can be described then as metamotivated, or unmotivated (if deficiencies are seen as the only motivations). It can also be described as self-actualizing, Being, expressing, rather than coping. This state of Being, rather than of striving, is suspected to be synonymous with selfhood, with being "authentic," with being a person, with being fully human. The process of growth is the process of *becoming* a person. *Being* a person is different.

22. Immaturity can also be differentiated from maturity in terms of the cognitive capacities (and also in terms of the emotional capacities). Immature and mature cognition have been best described by Werner and Piaget. We can now add another differentiation, that between D-cognition and B-cognition (D = Deficiency, B = Being). D-cognition can be defined as the cognitions which are organized from the point of view of basic needs or deficiency-needs and their gratification and frustration. That is, D-cognition could be called selfish cognition, in which the world is organized into gratifiers and frustrators of our own needs, with other characteristics being ignored or slurred. The cognition of the object, in its own right and its own Being, without reference to its need-gratifying or need-frustrating qualities, that is, without primary reference to its value for the observer or its effects upon him, can be called B-cognition (or self-

transcending, or unselfish, or objective cognition). The parallel with maturity is by no means perfect (children can also cognize in a selfless way), but in general, it is mostly true that with increasing selfhood or firmness of personal identity (or acceptance of one's own inner nature) B-cognition becomes easier and more frequent (This is true even though D-cognition remains for *all* human beings, including the mature ones, the main tool for living-in-the-world.)

To the extent that perception is desire-less and fearless, to that extent is it more veridical, in the sense of perceiving the true, or essential or intrinsic whole nature of the object (without splitting it up by abstraction). Thus the goal of objective and true description of any reality is fostered by psychological health. Neurosis, psychosis, stunting of growth—all are, from this point of view, cognitive diseases as well, contaminating perception, learning, remembering, attending and thinking.

23. A by-product of this aspect of cognition is a better understanding of the higher and lower levels of love. D-love can be differentiated from B-love on approximately the same basis as D-cognition and B-cognition, or D-motivation and B-motivation. No ideally good relation to another human being, especially a child, is possible without B-love. Especially is it necessary for teaching, along with the Taoistic, trusting attitude that it implies. This is also true for our relations with the natural world, i.e., we can treat it in its own right, or we can treat it as if it were there only for our purposes.

24. Though, in principle, self-actualization is easy, in practice it rarely happens (by my criteria, certainly in less than 1% of the adult population). For this, there are many, many reasons at various levels of discourse, including all the determinants of psychopathology that we now know. We have already mentioned one main cultural reason, i.e., the conviction that man's intrinsic nature is evil or dangerous, and one biological determinant for the difficulty of achieving a mature self, namely that humans no longer have strong instincts which tell them unequivocally what to do, when, where and how.

There is a subtle but extremely important difference between regarding psychopathology as blocking or evasion or fear of growth toward self-actualization, and thinking of it in a medical fashion, as akin to invasion from without by tumors, poisons or bacteria, which have no relationship to the personality being invaded. Human diminution (the loss of human potentialities and capacities) is a more useful concept than "illness" for our theoretical purposes.

25. Growth has not only rewards and pleasures but also many intrinsic pains and always will have. Each step forward is a step into the unfamiliar and is possibly dangerous. It also means giving up something familiar and good and satisfying. It frequently means a parting and a separation, even a kind of death prior to rebirth, with consequent nostalgia, fear, loneliness and mourning. It also often means giving up a simpler and easier and less effortful life, in exchange for a more demanding, more responsible, more difficult life. Growth forward *is in spite* of these losses and therefore requires courage, will, choice, and strength in the individual, as well as protection, permission and encouragement from the environment, especially for the child.

26. It is therefore useful to think of growth or lack of it as the resultant of a dialectic between growth-fostering forces and growth-discouraging forces (regression, fear, pains of growth, ignorance, etc.). Growth has both advantages and disadvantages. Non-growing has not only disadvantages, but also advantages. The future pulls, but so also does the past. There is not only courage but also fear. The total ideal way of growing healthily is, in principle, to enhance all the advantages of forward growth and all the disadvantages of not-growing, and to diminish all the disadvantages of growth forward and all the advantages of not-growing.

Homeostatic tendencies, "need-reduction" tendencies, and Freudian defense mechanisms are not growth-tendencies but are often defensive, pain-reducing postures of the organism. But they are quite necessary and not always pathological. They are generally prepotent over growth-tendencies.

27. All this implies a naturalistic system of values, a by-product of the empirical description of the deepest tendencies of the human species and of specific individuals. The study of the human being by science or by self-search can discover where he is heading, what is his purpose in life, what is good for him and what is bad for him, what will make him feel virtuous and what will make him feel guilty, why choosing the good is often difficult for him, what the attractions of evil are. (Observe that the word "ought" need not be used. Also such knowledge of man is relative to man only and does not purport to be "absolute.")

28. A neurosis is not part of the inner core but rather a defense against or an evasion of it, as well as a distorted expression of it (under the aegis of fear). It is ordinarily a compromise between the effort to seek basic need gratifications in a covert or disguised or self-defeating way, and the fear of these needs,

gratifications and motivated behaviors. To express neurotic needs, emotions, attitudes, definitions, actions, etc., means *not* to express the inner core or real self fully. If the sadist or exploiter or pervert says, "Why shouldn't I express myself?" (e.g., by killing), or, "Why shouldn't I actualize myself?" the answer to them is that such expression is a denial of, and not an expression of, instinctoid tendencies (or inner core).

Each neuroticized need, or emotion or action is a *loss of capacity* to the person, something that he cannot do or *dare* not do except in a sneaky and unsatisfying way. In addition, he has usually lost his subjective well-being, his will, and his feeling of self-control, his capacity for pleasure, his self-esteem, etc. He is diminished as a human being.

29. The state of being without a system of values is psychopathogenic, we are learning. The human being needs a framework of values, a philosophy of life, a religion or religion-surrogate to live by and understand by, in about the same sense that he needs sunlight, calcium or love. This I have called the "cognitive need to understand." The value-illnesses which result from valuelessness are called variously anhedonia, anomie, apathy, amorality, hopelessness, cynicism, etc., and can become somatic illness as well. Historically, we are in a value interregnum in which all externally given value systems have proven to be failures (political, economic, religious, etc.) e.g., nothing is worth dying for. What man needs but doesn't have, he seeks for unceasingly, and he becomes dangerously ready to jump at *any* hope, good or bad. The cure for this disease is obvious. We need a validated, usable system of human values that we can believe in and devote ourselves to (be willing to die for), because they are true rather than because we are exhorted to "believe and have faith." Such an empirically based Weltanschauung seems now to be a real possibility, at least in theoretical outline.

Much disturbance in children and adolescents can be understood as a consequence of the uncertainty of adults about their values. As a consequence, many youngsters in the United States live not by adult values but by adolescent values, which of course are immature, ignorant and heavily determined by confused adolescent needs. An excellent projection of these adolescent values is the cowboy, "Western" movie, or the delinquent gang.

30. At the level of self-actualizing, many dichotomies become resolved, opposites are seen to be unities and the whole dichotomous way of thinking is recognized to be immature. For self-actualizing people, there is a strong tendency for selfishness and unselfishness to fuse into a higher, superordinate

unity. Work tends to be the same as play; vocation and avocation become the same thing. When duty is pleasant and pleasure is fulfillment of duty, then they lose their separateness and oppositeness. The highest maturity is discovered to include a childlike quality, and we discover healthy children to have some of the qualities of mature self-actualization. The inner-outer split, between self and all else, gets fuzzy and much less sharp, and they are seen to be permeable to each other at the highest levels of personality development. Dichotomizing seems now to be characteristic of a lower level of personality development and of psychological functioning; it is both a cause and an effect of psychopathology.

31. One especially important finding in self-actualizing people is that they tend to integrate the Freudian dichotomies and trichotomies, i.e., the conscious, preconscious and the unconscious, (as well as id, ego, superego). The Freudian "instincts" and the defenses are less sharply set off against each other. The impulses are more expressed and less controlled; the controls are less rigid, inflexible, anxiety-determined. The superego is less harsh and punishing and less set off against the ego. The primary and secondary cognitive processes are more equally available and more equally valued (instead of the primary processes being stigmatized as pathological). Indeed, in the "peak-experience" the walls between them tend to fall together.

This is in sharp contrast with the early Freudian position in which these various forces were sharply dichotomized as (a) mutually exclusive, (b) with antagonistic interests, i.e., as antagonistic forces rather than as complementary or collaborating ones, and (c) one "better" than the other.

Again we imply here (sometimes) a healthy unconscious, and desirable regression. Furthermore, we imply also an integration of rationality and irrationality with the consequence that irrationality may, in its place, also be considered healthy, desirable or even necessary.

32. Healthy people are more integrated in another way. In them the conative, the cognitive, the affective and the motor are less separated from each other, and are more synergic, i.e., working collaboratively without conflict to the same ends. The conclusions of rational, careful thinking are apt to come to the same conclusions as those of the blind appetites. What such a person wants and enjoys is apt to be just what is good for him. His spontaneous reactions are as capable, efficient and right as if they had been thought out in advance. His sensory and motor reactions are more closely correlated. His sensory modalities are more connected with each other (physiognomical

perception). Furthermore, we have learned the difficulties and dangers of those age-old rationalistic systems in which the capacities were thought to be arranged dichotomously-hierarchically, with rationality at the top, rather than in an integration.

33. This development toward the concept of a healthy unconscious, and of a healthy irrationality, sharpens our awareness of the limitations of purely abstract thinking, of verbal thinking and of analytic thinking. If our hope is to describe the world fully, a place is necessary for pre-verbal, ineffable, metaphorical, primary process, concrete-experience, intuitive and esthetic types of cognition, for there are certain aspects of reality which can be cognized in no other way. Even in science this is true, now that we know (1) that creativity has its roots in the non-rational, (2) that language is and must always be inadequate to describe total reality, (3) that any abstract concept leaves out much of reality, and (4) that what we call "knowledge" (which is usually highly abstract and verbal and sharply defined) often serves to blind us to those portions of reality not covered by the abstraction. That is, it makes us more able to see some things, but *less* able to see other things. Abstract knowledge has its dangers as well as its uses.

Science and education, being too exclusively abstract, verbal and bookish, don't have enough place for raw, concrete, esthetic experience, especially of the subjective happenings inside oneself. For instance, organismic psychologists would certainly agree on the desirability of more creative education in perceiving and creating art, in dancing, in (Greek style) athletics and in phenomenological observation.

The ultimate of abstract, analytical thinking, is the greatest simplification possible, i.e., the formula, the diagram, the map, the blueprint, the schema, the cartoon, and certain types of abstract paintings. Our mastery of the world is enhanced thereby, but its richness may be lost as a forfeit, *unless* we learn to value B-cognitions, perception-with-love-and-care, free-floating attention, all of which enrich the experience instead of impoverishing it. There is no reason why "science" should not be expanded to include both kinds of knowing.

34. This ability of healthier people to dip into the unconscious and preconscious, to use and value their primary processes instead of fearing them, to accept their impulses instead of always controlling them, to be able to regress voluntarily without fear, turns out to be one of the main conditions of creativity. We can then understand why psychological health is so closely tied

up with certain universal forms of creativeness (aside from special-talent), as to lead some writers to make them almost synonymous.

This same tie between health and integration of rational and irrational forces (conscious and unconscious, primary and secondary processes) also permits us to understand why psychologically healthy people are more able to enjoy, to love, to laugh, to have fun, to be humorous, to be silly, to be whimsical and fantastic, to be pleasantly "crazy," and in general to permit and value and enjoy emotional experiences in general and peak experiences in particular and to have them more often. And it leads us to the strong suspicion that learning *ad hoc* to be able to do all these things may help the child move toward health.

35. Esthetic perceiving and creating and esthetic peak-experiences are seen to be a central aspect of human life and of psychology and education rather than a peripheral one. This is true for several reasons. (1) All the peak-experiences are (among other characteristics) integrative of the splits within the person, between persons, within the world, and between the person and the world. Since one aspect of health is integration, the peak-experiences are moves toward health and are themselves, momentary healths. (2) These experiences are life-validating, i.e., they make life worth while. These are certainly an important part of the answer to the question, "Why don't we all commit suicide?" (3) They are worth while in themselves, etc.

36. Self-actualization does not mean a transcenaence of all human problems. Conflict, anxiety, frustration, sadness, hurt, and guilt can all be found in healthy human beings. In general, the movement, with increasing maturity, is from neurotic pseudo-problems to the real, unavoidable, existential problems, inherent in the nature of man (even at his best) living in a particular kind of world. Even though he is not neurotic he may be troubled by real, desirable and necessary guilt rather than neurotic guilt (which isn't desirable or necessary), by an intrinsic conscience (rather than the Freudian superego). Even though he has transcended the problems of Becoming, there remain the problems of Being. To be untroubled when one *should* be troubled can be a sign of sickness. Sometimes, smug people have to be scared "*into* their wits."

37. Self-actualization is not altogether general. It takes place via femaleness *or* maleness, which are prepotent to general-humanness. That is, one must first be a healthy, femaleness-fulfilled woman or maleness-fulfilled man before general-human self-actualization becomes possible.

There is also a little evidence that different constitutional types actualize themselves in somewhat different ways (because they have different inner selves to actualize).

38. Another crucial aspect of healthy growth of selfhood and full-humanness is dropping away the techniques used by the child, in his weakness and smallness for adapting himself to the strong, large, all-powerful, omniscient, godlike adults. He must replace these with the techniques of being strong and independent and of being a parent himself. This involves especially giving up the child's desperate wish for the exclusive, total love of his parents while learning to love others. He must learn to gratify his own needs and wishes, rather than the needs of his parents, and he must learn to gratify them himself, rather than depending upon the parents to do this for him. He must give up being good out of fear and in order to keep their love, and must be good because *he* wishes to be. He must discover his own conscience and give up his internalized parents as a sole ethical guide. All these techniques by which weakness adapts itself to strength are necessary for the child but immature and stunting in the adult (103). He must replace fear with courage.

39. From this point of view, a society or a culture can be either growth-fostering or growth-inhibiting. The sources of growth and of humanness are essentially within the human person and are not created or invented by society, which can only help or hinder the development of humanness, just as a gardener can help or hinder the growth of a rosebush, but cannot determine that it shall be an oak tree. This is true even though we know that a culture is a *sine qua non* for the actualization of humanness itself, e.g., language, abstract thought, ability to love; but these exist as potentialities in human germ plasm prior to culture.

This makes theoretically possible a comparative sociology, transcending and including cultural relativity. The "better" culture gratifies all basic human needs and permits self-actualization. The "poorer" cultures do not. The same is true for education. To the extent that it fosters growth toward self-actualization, it is "good" education.

As soon as we speak of "good" or "bad" cultures, and take them as means rather than as ends, the concept of "adjustment" comes into question. We must ask, "What kind of culture or subculture is the 'well adjusted' person well adjusted *to*?" Adjustment is, very definitely, *not* necessarily synonymous with psychological health.

Q40. The achievement of self-actualization (in the sense of autonomy) paradoxically makes *more* possible the transcendence of self, and of self-consciousness and of selfishness. It makes it *easier* for the person to be homonomous, i.e., to merge himself as a part in a larger whole than himself (6). The condition of the fullest homonomy is full autonomy, and to some extent, vice versa, one can attain to autonomy only via successful homonomous experiences (child dependence, B-love, care for others, etc.). It is necessary to speak of levels of homonomy (more and more mature), and to differentiate a "low homonomy" (of fear, weakness, and regression) from a "high homonomy" (of courage and full, self-confident autonomy), a "low Nirvana" from a" high Nirvana, union downward from union upward (170).

41. An important existential problem is posed by the fact that self-actualizing persons (and *all* people in their peak-experiences) occasionally live out-of-time and out-of-the-world (atemporal and aspatial) even though mostly they *must* live in the outer world. Living in the inner psychic world (which is ruled by psychic laws and not by the laws of outer-reality), i.e., the world of experience, of emotion, of wishes and fears and hopes, of love, of poetry, art, and fantasy, is different from living in and adapting to the non-psychic reality which runs by laws he never made and which are not essential to his nature even though he has to live by them. (He *could*, after all, live in other kinds of worlds, as any science fiction fan knows.) The person who is not afraid of this inner, psychic world, can enjoy it to such an extent that it may be called Heaven by contrast with the more effortful, fatiguing, externally responsible world of "reality," of striving and coping, of right and wrong, of truth and falsehood. This is true even though the healthier person can also adapt more easily and enjoyably to the "real" world, and has better "reality testing," i.e., doesn't confuse it with his inner psychic world.

It seems clear now that confusing these inner and outer realities, or having either closed off from experience, is highly pathological. The healthy person is able to integrate them both into his life and therefore has to give up neither, being able to go back and forth voluntarily. The difference is the same as the one between the person who can *visit* the slums and the one who is forced to live there always. (*Either* world is a slum if one can't leave it.) Then, paradoxically, that which was sick and pathological and the "lowest" becomes part of the healthiest and "highest" aspect of human nature. Slipping into "craziness" is frightening only for those who are not fully confident of their sanity. Education must help the person to live in both worlds.

42. The foregoing propositions generate a different understanding of the role of action in psychology. Goal-directed, motivated, coping, striving, purposeful action is an aspect or by-product of the necessary transactions between a psyche and a non-psychic world.

(a) The D-need gratifications come from the world outside the person, not from within. Therefore adaptation to this world is made necessary, e.g., reality-testing, knowing the nature of this world, learning to differentiate this world from the inner world, learning the nature of people and of society, learning to delay gratification, learning to conceal what would be dangerous, learning which portions of the world are gratifying and which dangerous, or useless for need-gratification, learning the approved and permitted cultural paths to gratification and techniques of gratification.

(b) The world is in itself interesting, beautiful and fascinating. Exploring it, manipulating it, playing with it, contemplating it, enjoying it are all motivated kinds of action (cognitive, motor, and esthetic needs).

But there is also action which has little or nothing to do with the world, at any rate at first. Sheer expression of the nature or state or powers (Funktionslust) of the organism is an expression of Being rather than of striving (24). And the contemplation and enjoyment of the inner life not only is a kind of "action" in itself but is also antithetical to action in the world, i.e., it produces stillness and cessation of muscular activity. The ability to wait is a special case of being able to suspend action.

43. From Freud we learned that the past exists *now* in the person. Now we must learn, from growth theory and self-actualization theory that the future also *now* exists in the person in the form of ideals, hopes, duties, tasks, plans, goals, unrealized potentials, mission, fate, destiny, etc. One for whom no future exists is reduced to the concrete, to hopelessness, to emptiness. For him, time must be endlessly "filled." Striving, the usual organizer of most activity, when lost, leaves the person unorganized and unintegrated.

Of course, being in a state of Being needs no future, because it is already *there*. Then Becoming ceases for the moment and its promissory notes are cashed in the form of the ultimate rewards, i.e., the peak-experiences, in which time disappears and hopes are fulfilled.

Appendix A

Are Our Publications and Conventions Suitable for the Personal Psychologies?₂[1]

A few weeks ago, I suddenly saw how I could integrate some aspects of Gestalt theory with my health-and-growth psychology. One after another, problems that had tantalized me for years all solved themselves. It was a typical instance of a peak-experience, rather more extended than most. The rumblings after the main storm (the working through) continued for days, as one implication after another of the original insights came to mind. Since it is my custom to think on paper, I have the whole thing written out. My temptation then was to throw away the rather professorial paper I was preparing for this meeting. Here was an *actual*, living peak-experience caught on the wing, and it illustrated very nicely ("in color") the various points I was going to make about the acute or poignant "identity-experience."

And yet because it was so private and so unconventional, I found myself extremely reluctant to read this out loud in public and am not going to.

However the self-analysis of this reluctance has made me aware of some things that I do want to talk about. The realization that this kind of paper didn't "fit," either for publication or for presentation at conventions or conferences, led to the question, "Why doesn't it fit?" What is there about intellectual meetings and scientific journals that makes certain kinds of personal truth and certain styles of expression not "suitable" or appropriate?

The answer that I have come to *is* quite appropriate for discussion here. We are groping in this meeting toward the phenomenological, the experiential, the existential, the ideographic, the unconscious, the private, the acutely personal; but it has become clear to me that we are trying to do this in an inherited intellectual atmosphere or framework which is quite unsuitable and unsympathetic, one which I might even call forbidding.

Our journals, books and conferences are primarily suitable for the communication and discussion of the rational, the abstract, the logical, the public, the impersonal, the nomothetic, the repeatable, the objective, the unemotional. They thereby assume the very things that we "personal psychologists" are trying to change. In other words, they beg the question. One result is that as therapists or as self-observers we are still forced by academic custom to talk about our own experiences or those of patients in about the same way as we might talk about bacteria, or about the moon, or about white rats, *assuming* the subject-object cleavage, *assuming* that we are detached, distant and uninvolved, *assuming* that we (and the objects of perception) are unmoved and unchanged by the act of observation, *assuming* that we can split off the "I" from the "Thou," *assuming* that all observation, thinking, expression and communication must be cool and never warm, *assuming* that cognition can only be contaminated or distorted by emotion, etc.

In a word, we keep trying to use the canons and folkways of impersonal science for our personal science, but I am convinced that this won't work. It is also quite clear to me now that the scientific revolution that some of us are cooking up (as we construct a philosophy of science large enough to include experiential knowledge) must extend itself to the folkways of intellectual communication as well.

We must make explicit what we all accept implicitly, that our kind of work is often felt deeply and comes out of deep personal grounds, that we sometimes fuse with the objects of study rather than splitting from them, that we are usually profoundly involved, and that we *must* be if our work is not to be fake. We must also accept honestly and express candidly the profound truth that most of our "objective" work is simultaneously subjective, that our outer world is frequently isomorphic with our inner world, that the "external problems" we deal with "scientifically" are often also our own internal problems, and that our solutions to these problems are also, in principle, self-therapies in the broadest sense.

This is more *acutely* true for us, the personal scientists, but in principle it is true for all impersonal scientists as well. Looking for order, law, control, predictability, grasp-ability in the stars and plants is often isomorphic with the search for *inner* law, control, etc. Impersonal science can sometimes be a flight from or defense against, inner disorder and chaos, against the fear of loss of control. Or, to put it more generally, impersonal science can be (and often enough *is*, I have found) a flight from or defense against the personal within oneself and within other human beings, a distaste for emotion and impulse, even sometimes a disgust with humanness or a fear of it.

It is obviously foolish to try to do the work of personal science in a framework which is based on the very negation of what we are discovering. We cannot hope to work toward non-Aristotelianism by using a strictly Aristotelian framework. We can not move toward experiential knowledge using only the tool of abstraction. Similarly, subject-object separation discourages fusion. Dichotomizing forbids integrating. Respecting the rational, verbal, and logical as the *only* language of truth inhibits us in our necessary study of the non-rational, of the poetic, the mythic, the vague, the primary process, the dreamlike.[2] The classical, impersonal and objective methods which have worked so well for some problems, *don't* work well for these newer, scientific problems.

We must help the "scientific" psychologists to realize that they are working on the basis of *a* philosophy of science, not *the* philosophy of science, and that *any* philosophy of science which serves primarily an excluding function is a set of blinders, a handicap rather than a help. *All* the world, *all* of experience must be open to study. *Nothing,* not even the "personal" problems, need be closed off from human investigation. Otherwise we will force ourselves into the idiotic position that some labor unions have frozen themselves into; where only carpenters may touch wood, and carpenters may touch only wood. New materials and new methods must then be annoying and even threatening, catastrophes rather than opportunities. I remind you also of the primitive tribes who must place everyone in the kinship system. If a newcomer shows up who cannot be placed, there is no way to solve the problem but to kill him.

I know that these remarks may be easily misunderstood as an attack upon science. They are not. Rather I am suggesting that we enlarge the jurisdiction of science so as to include within its realm the problems and the data of personal and experiential psychology. Many scientists have abdicated from these problems, considering them "unscientific." Leaving them to non-scientists, however, supports that separation of the world of science from the world of the "humanities" which is now crippling them both.

As for new kinds of communication, it is difficult to guess exactly what must come. Certainly we must have more of what we already find occasionally in the psychoanalytic literature, namely, the discussion of the transference and the counter-transference. We must accept more ideographic papers for our journals, both biographical and autobiographical. Long ago, John Dollard prefaced his book on the South with an analysis of his own prejudices; we must learn to do this too. We certainly should have more reports of the lessons learned from psychotherapy by the "therapped" people themselves, more self-analyses like Marion Milner's *On Not Being Able To Paint,* more case histories like those written by Eugenia Hanfmann, more verbatim reports of all sorts of interpersonal contacts.

Most difficult of all, however, judging by my own inhibitions, will be gradually opening up our journals to papers written in rhapsodic, poetic or free association style. Some communication of some kinds of truth is best done in this way, e.g., any of the peak-experiences. Nevertheless, this is going to be hard on everybody. The most astute editors would be needed for the terrible job of separating out the scientifically useful from the great flood of trash that would surely come as soon as this door was opened. All I can suggest is a cautious trying out.

Appendix B

Bibliography

This bibliography includes not only specific references made in the text, but also a sampling of writings by the "Third Force" group of writers in psychology and psychiatry. The best introduction to their writings is Moustakas (118). Good general texts presenting this point of view are Jourard (72) and Coleman (33).

1. ALLPORT, G. *The Nature of Personality.* Addison-Wesley, 1950.
2. *Becoming.* Yale Univ., 1955.
3. . Normative compatibility in the light of social science, in Maslow, A. H. (ed.). New *Knowledge in Human Values.* Harper, 1959.
4. *Personality and Social Encounter.* Beacon, 1960.
5. ANDERSON, H. H. (ed.). *Creativity and Its Cultivation.* Harper, 1959.
6. ANGYAL, A. *Foundations for a Science of Personality.* Commonwealth Fund, 1941.
7. Anonymous, Finding the real self. A letter with a foreword by Karen Horney, *Amer. J. Psychoanal.,* 1949, 9, 3.
8. ANSBACHER, H., and R. *The Individual Psychology of Alfred Adler.* Basic Books, 1956.
9. ARNOLD, M., and GASSON, J. *The Human Person.* Ronald, 1954.
10. ASCH, S. E. *Social Psychology.* Prentice-Hall, 1952.
11. ASSAGIOLI, R. *Self-Realization and Psychological Disturbances.* Psychosynthesis Research Foundation, 1961.
12. BANKAM, K. M. The development of affectionate behavior in infancy, *J. General Pyschol,* 1950, 76, 283-289.
13. BARRETT, W. *Irrational Man.* Doubleday, 1958.
14. BARTLETT, F. C. *Remembering.* Cambridge Univ., 1932.
15. BEGBIE, H. *Twice Born Men.* Revell, 1909.
16. BETTELHEIM, B. *The Informed Heart.* Free Press, 1960.
16a. BOSSOM, J., and MASLOW, A. H. Security of judges as a factor in impressions of warmth in others, *J. Abn. Soc. Psychol.,* 1957, 55, 147-148.
17. BOWLBY, J. *Maternal Care and Mental Health.* Geneva:World Health Organization, 1952.

18. BRONOWSKI, J. The values of science *in* Maslow, A. H. (ed.). *New Knowledge in Human Values.* Harper, 1959.

19. BROWN, N. *Life Against Death.* Random House, 1959.

20. BUBER, M. *I and Thou.* Edinburgh: T. and T. Clark, 1937.

21. BUCKE, R. *Cosmic Consciousness.* Dutton, 1923.

22. BUHLET, C. Maturation and motivation, *Dialectica,* 1951, 5, 312-361.

23. The reality principle, *Amer.]. Psychother.,* 1954, 8, 626-647.

24. BUHLER, K. *Die geistige Entwickling des Kindes,* 4th ed., Jena: Fischer, 1924.

25. BURTT, E. A. (ed.). *The Teachings of the Compassionate Buddha.* Mentor Books, 1955.

26. BYRD, B. Cognitive needs and human motivation. Unpublished.

27. CANNON, W. B. *Wisdom of the Body.* Norton, 1932.

28. CANTRIL, H. *The "Why" of Man's Experience.* Macmillan, 1950.

29. CANTRIL, H., and BUMSTEAD, C. *Reflections on the Human Venture.* N. Y. Univ., 1960.

30. CLUTTON-BROCK, A. *The Ultimate Belief.* Dutton, 1916.

31. COHEN, S. A growth theory of neurotic resistance to psychotherapy, *J. of Humanistic Psychol.,* 1961, 1, 48-63.

32. Neurotic ambiguity and neurotic hiatus between knowledge and action, *J.. Existential Psychiatry,* in press.

33. COLEMAN, J. *Personality Dynamics and Effective Behavior.* Scott, Foresman, 1960.

34. COMBS, A., and SNYGG, D. *Individual Behavior.* Harper, 1959.

35. COMBS, A. (ed.). *Perceiving, Behaving, Becoming: A NewFocus for Education.* Association for Supervision and Curriculum Development, Washington D.C., 1962.

36. D'ARCY, M. C. *The Mind and Heart of Love.* Holt, 1947.

37. The Meeting of Love and Knowledge. Harper, 1957.

38. DEUTSCH, F., and MURPHY, W. *The Clinical Interview* (2 vols.). Int. Univs. Press, 1955.

38a. DEWEY, J. *Theory of Valuation.* Vol. II, No. 4 of *International Encyclopedia of Unified Science,* Univ. of Chicago (undated).

38b. DOVE, W. F. A study of individuality in the nutritive instincts, *Amer. Naturalist,* 1935, 69, 469-544.

39. EHRENZWEIG, A. *The Psychoanalysis of Artistic Vision and Hearing.* Routledge, 1953.

40. ERIKSON, E. H. *Childhood and Society.* Norton, 1950.

41. ERISKON, H. Identity and The Life Cycle. (Selected papers.) *Psychol. Issues,* 1, Monograph 1, 1959. Int. Univs. Press.

42. FESTINGER, L. A. *Theory of Cognitive Dissonance.* Peterson, 1957.

43. FEUER, L. *Psychoanalysis and Ethics.* Thomas, 1955. FIELD, J. (pseudonym), *see* MILNER, M.

44. FRANKL, V. E. *The Doctor and the Soul.* Knopf, 1955.

45. From *Death-Camp to Existentialism. Beacon,* 1959.

46. FREUD, S. *Beyond the Pleasure Principle.* Int. Psychoan. Press, 1922.

47. The Interpretation of Dreams, in *The Basic Writings of Freud.* Modern Lib., 1938.

48. Collected Papers, London, Hogarth, 1956. Vol. III, Vol. IV.

49. An *Outline of Psychoanalysis.* Norton, 1949.

50. FROMM, E. *Man For Himself.* Rinehart, 1947.

51. Psychoanalysis and Religion. Yale Univ., 1950.

52. The Forgotten Language. Rinehart, 1951.

53. The Sane Society. Rinehart, 1955.

54. Suzuki, D. T., and DE MARTINO, R. Zen *Buddhism and Psychoanalysis.* Harper, 1960.

54a. GHISELIN, B. *The Creative Process,* Univ. of Calif., 1952.

55. GOLDSTEIN, K. *The Organism.* Am. Bk. Co., 1939.

56. *Human Nature from the Point of View of Psychopathology.* Harvard Univ., 1940.

57. Health as value, *in* A. H. Maslow (ed.). *New Knowledge in Human Values.* Harper, 1959, pp. 178-188.

58. HALMOS, P. *Towards A Measure of Man.* London: Kegan Paul, 1957.

59. HARTMAN, R. The science of value, *in* Maslow, A. H. (ed.). *New Knowledge in Human Values.* Harper, 1959.

60. HARTMANN, H. Ego *Psychology and the Problem of Adaptation.* Int. Univs. Press, 1958.

61. *Psychoanalysis and Moral Values.* Int. Univs. Press, 1960.

62. HAYAKAWA, S. I. *Language in Action.* Harcourt, 1942.

63. The fully functioning personality, ETC. 1956, 13, 164-181.

64. HEBB, D. O., & THOMPSON, W. R. The social significance of animal studies, *in* G. Lindzey (ed.). *Handbook of Social Psychology, Vol. 1.* Addison-Wesley, 1954, 532-561.

65. HILL, W. E. Activity as an autonomous drive, *J. Comp.& Physiological Psychol.,* 1956, 49,15-19.

66. HORA, T. Existential group psychotherapy, *Amer. J. of Psychotherapy,* 1959, 13, 83-92.

67. HORNEY, K. *Neurosis and Human Growth.* Norton, 1950.

68. HUIZINCA, J. *Homo Ludens.* Beacon, 1950.

68a. HUXLEY, A. *The Perennial Philosophy.* Harper, 1944.

69. *Heaven & Hell.* Harper, 1955.

70. JAHODA, M. *Current Conceptions of Positive Mental Health.* Basic Books, 1958.

70a. JAMES, W. *The Varieties of Religious Experience.* Modern Lib., 1942.

71. JESSNER, L., and KAPLAN, S. "Discipline" as a problem in psychotherapy with children, *The Nervous Child,* 1951, 9, 147-155.

72. JOURARD, S. M. *Personal Adjustment.* Macmillan, 1958.

73. JUNG, C. G. *Modern Man in Search of a Soul.* Harcourt, 1933.

74. *Psychological Reflections* (Jacobi, J., ed.). Pantheon Books, 1953.

75. *The Undiscovered Self.* London: Kegan Paul, London, 1958.

76. KARPF, F. B. *The Psychology & Psychotherapy of Otto Rank.* Philosophical Library, 1953.

77. KAUFMAN, W. *Existentialism from Dostoevsky to Sartre.* Meridian, 1956.

78.*Nietzsche.* Meridian, 1956.

79. KEPES, G. *The New Landscape in Art and Science.* Theobald, 1957.

80. The *Journals of Kierkegaard,* 1834-1854. Dru, Alexander, (ed. and translator). Fontana Books, 1958.

81. KLEE, J. B. *The Absolute and the Relative.* Unpublished.

82. KLUCKHOHN, C. *Mirror for Man.* McGraw-Hill, 1949.

83. KORZYBSKI, A. *Science and Sanity: An Introduction to Non-Aristotelian Systems and General Semantics* (1933). Lakeville, Conn.: International Non-Aristotelian Lib. Pub. Co., 3rd ed., 1948.

84. KRIS, E. Psychoanalytic *Explorations in Art,* Int. Univs. Press, 1952.

85. KRISHNAMURTI, J. *The First and Last Freedom.* Harper, 1954.

86. KUBIE, L, S. *Neurotic Distortion of the Creative Process.* Univ. of Kans., 1958.

87. KUENZLI, A. E. (ed.). *The Phenomenological Problem.* Harper, 1959.

88. LEE, D. *Freedom & Culture.* A Spectrum Book, Prentice-Hall, 1959.

89. Autonomous motivation, *J. Humanistic Psychol.,* in press.

90. LEVY D. M. Personal communication.

91. *Maternal Overprotection.* Columbia Univ., 1943.

91a. LEWIS, C. S. *Surprised by Joy.* Harcourt, 1956.

92. LYND, H. M. On *Shame and the Search for Identity.* Harcourt, 1958.

93. MARCUSE, H. Eros *and Civilization.* Beacon, 1955.

94. MASLOW, A. H., and MITTELMANN, B. *Principles of Abnormal Psychology.* Harper, 1941.

95. MASLOW, A. H. Experimentalizing the clinical method, *J. of Clinical Psychol,* 1945, 1, 241-243.

96. Resistance to acculturation, *J. Soc. Issues,* 1951, 7, 26-29.

96a. Comments on Dr. Old's paper, *in* M. R. Jones (ed.). *Nebraska Symposium on Motivation,* 1955, Univ. of Neb., 1955.

97. Motivation and *Personality.* Harper, 1954.

98. A philosophy of psychology, *in* Fairchild, J. (ed.). *Personal Problems and Psychological Frontiers.* Sheridan, 1957.

99. Power relationships and patterns of personal development, *in* Kornhauser, A. (ed.). *Problems of Power in American Democracy.* Wayne Univ., 1957.

100. Two kinds of cognition, *General Semantics Bulletin,* 1957, Nos. 20 and 21, 17-22.

101. Emotional blocks to creativity, *J. Individ. Psychol,* 1958, 14, 51-56.

102. (ed.). New Knowledge *in Human Values.* Harper, 1959.

103. Rand, H., and NEWMAN, S. Some parallels between the dominance and sexual behavior of monkeys and the fantasies of psychoanalytic patients, *J. of Nervous and Mental Disease,* 1960, 131, 202-212.

104. Lessons from the peak-experiences, *J. Humanistic Psychol.,* in press.

105. DIAZ-GUERRERO, R. Juvenile delinquency as a value disturbance, in Peatman, J., and Hartley, E. (eds.). *Festschrift for Gardner Murphy.* Harper, 1960.

106. Peak-experiences as completions. (To be published.)

107. Eupsychia, *J. Humanistic Psychol.* (To be published.)

108. and MINTZ, N. L. Effects of esthetic surroundings: I. Initial shortterm effects of three esthetic conditions upon perceiving "energy" and "well-being" in faces, *J. Psychol.,* 1956, 41, 247-254.

109. MASSERMAN, J. (ed.). *Psychoanalysis and Human Values.* Grune and Stratton, 1960.

110. MAY, R., et al (eds.). *Existence.* Basic Books, 1958.

111. (ed.). *Existential Psychology.* Random House, 1961.

112. MILNER, M. (Joanna Field, pseudonym). A *Life of One's Own.* Pelican Books, 1952.

113. MILNER, M. *On Not Being Able to Paint.* Int. Univs. Press, 1957.

114. MINTZ, N. L. Effects of esthetic surroundings: II. Prolonged and repeated experiences in a "beautiful" and an "ugly" room. *J. Psychol,* 1956, 41, 459-466.

115. MONTAGU, ASHLEY, M. F. *The Direction of Human Development.* Harper, 1955.

115a. MORENO, J. (ed.). *Sociometry Reader.* Free Press, 1960.

116. MORRIS, C. *Varieties of Human Value.* Univ. of Chicago, 1956.

117. MOUSTAKAS, C. *The Teacher and the Child.* McGraw-Hill, 1956.

118. (ed.). *The Self.* Harper, 1956.

119. MOWRER, O. H. *The Crisis in Psychiatry and Religion.* Van Nostrand, 1961.

120. MUMFORD, L. *The Transformations of Man.* Harper, 1956.

121. MUNROE, R. L. *Schools of Psychoanalytic Thought.* Dryden, 1955.

122. MURPHY, G. *Personality.* Harper, 1947.

123. MURPHY, G., and HOCHBERG, J. Perceptual development: some tentative hypotheses, *Psychol. Rev.,* 1951, 58, 332-349.

124. MURPHY, G. *Human Potentialities.* Basic Books, 1958.

125. MURRAY, H. A. Vicissitudes of Creativity, *in* H. H. Anderson (ed.). *Creativity and Its Cultivation.* Harper, 1959.

126. NAMECHE, G. Two pictures of man, *J. Humanistic Psychol.,* 1961, 1, 70-88.

127. NIEBUHR, R. *The Nature and Destiny of Man.* Scribner's, 1947.

127a. NORTHROP, F. C. S. *The Meeting of East and West.* Macmillan, 1946.

128. NUTTIN, J. *Psychoanalysis and Personality.* Sheed and Ward, 1953.

129. O'CONNELL, V. On brain washing by psychotherapists: The effect of cognition in the relationship in psychotherapy. Mimeographed, 1960.

129a. OLDS, J. Physiological mechanisms of reward, *in* Jones, M. R. (ed.). *Nebraska Symposium on Motivation,* 1955. Univ. of Nebr., 1955.

130. OPPENHEIMER, O. Toward a new instinct theory, *J. Social Psychol,* 1958, 47, 21-31.

131. OVERSTREET, H. A. *The Mature Mind.* Norton, 1949.

132. OWENS, C. M. *Awakening to the Good.* Christopher, 1958.

133. PERLS, F., HEFFERLINE, R., and GOODMAN, P. *Gestalt Therapy.* Julian, 1951.

134. PETERS, R. S. "Mental health" as an educational aim. Paper read before Philosophy of Education Society, Harvard University, March, 1961.

135. PROGOFF, I. *Jung's Psychology and Its Social Meaning.* Grove, 1953.

136. PROGOFF, I. *Depth Psychology and Modern Man.* Julian, 1959.

137. RAPAPORT, D. *Organization and Pathology of Thought.* Columbia Univ., 1951.

138. REICH, W. *Character Analysis.* Orgone Inst., 1949.

139. REIK, T. *Of Love and Lust.* Farrar, Straus, 1957.

140. RIESMAN, D. *The Lonely Crowd.* Yale Univ., 1950.

141. RITCHIE, B. F. Comments on Professor Farber's paper, *in* Marshall R. Jones (ed.). *Nebraska Symposium on Motivation.* Univ. of Nebr., 1954, pp. 46-50.

142. ROGERS, C. *Psychotherapy and Personality Change.* Univ. of Chicago, 1954.

143. ROGERS, C. R. A theory of therapy, personality and interpersonal relationships as developed in the client-centered framework, in Koch, S. (ed.). *Psychology: A Study of a Science, Vol. III.* McGraw-Hill, 1959.

144. ROGERS, C. A *Therapist's View of Personal Goals.* Pendle Hill, 1960.

145. On Becoming a Person. Houghton Mifflin, 1961.

146. ROKEACH, M. *The Open and Closed Mind.* Basic Books, 1960.

147. SCHACHTEL, E. *Metamorphosis.* Basic Books, 1959.

148. SCHILDEK, P. *Goals and Desires of Man.* Columbia Univ., 1942.

149. Mind: Perception and Thought in Their Constructive Aspects. Columbia Univ., 1942.

150. SCHEINFELD, A. *The New You and Heredity.* Lippincott, 1950.

151. SCHWARZ, O. *The Psychology of Sex.* Pelican Books, 1951.

152. SHAW, F. J. The problem of acting and the problem of becoming, *J. Humanistic Psychol.,* 1961, 1, 64-69.

153. SHELDON, W. H. *The Varieties of Temperament.* Harper, 1942.

154. SHLIEN, J. M. *Creativity and Psychological Health.*Counseling Center Discussion Paper, 1956, 11, 1-6.

155. SHLIEN, J. M. A criterion of psychological health, *Group Psychotherapy,* 1956, 9, 1-18.

156. SINNOTT, E. W. *Matter, Mind and Man.* Harper, 1957.

157. SMILIEᴇ, D. Truth and reality from two points of view, in Moustakas, C, (ed.). *The Self.* Harper, 1956.

157a. SMITH, M. B. "Mental health" reconsidered: A special case of the problem of values in psychology, *Amer. Psychol.,* 1961, 16, 299-306.

158. SOROKIN, P. A. (ed.). *Explorations in Altruistic Love and Behavior.* Beacon, 1950.

159. S[ITZ, R. Anaclitic depression, *Psychoanal. Study of the Child,* 1946, 2, 313-342.

160. SUTTIE, I. *Origins of Love and Hate.* London: Kegan Paul, 1935.

160a. SZASZ, T. S. The myth of mental illness, *Amer. Psychol.,* 1960, 15, 113-118.

161. TAYLOR, C. (ed.). *Research Conference on the Identification of Creative Scientific Talent.* Univ. of Utah, 1956.

162. TEAD, O. Toward the knowledge of man, *Main Currents in Modern Thought,* Nov. 1955.

163. TILLICH, P. *The Courage To Be.* Yale Univ., 1952.

164. THOMPSON, C. *Psychoanalysis: Evolution & Development.* Grove, 1957.

165. VAN KAAM, A. L. *The Third Force in European Psychology—Its Expression in a Theory of Psychotherapy.* Psychosynthesis Research Foundation, 1960.

166. Phenomenal analysis: Exemplified by a study of the experience of "really feeling understood," *J. of Indiv. Psychol,* 1959, 15, 66-72.

167. Humanistic psychology and culture, J. *Humanistic Psychol,* 1961, 1, 94-100.

168. WATTS, A. W. *Nature, Man and Woman.* Pantheon, 1958.

169. This *is* IT. Pantheon, 1960.

170. WEISSKOPF, W. Existence and values, *in* Maslow, A. H. (ed.). New *Knowledge of Human Values.* Harper, 1958.

171. WERNER, H. *Comparative Psychology of Mental Development.* Harper, 1940.

172. WERTHEIMER, M. Unpublished lectures at the New School for Social Research, 1935-6.

173. *Productive Thinking.* Harper, 1959.

174. WHEELIS, A. *The Quest for Identity.* Norton, 1958.

175. The Seeker. Random, 1960.

176. WHITE, M. (ed.). *The Age of Analysis.* Mentor Books, 1957.

177. WHITE, R. Motivation reconsidered: the concept of competence, *Psychol. Rev.,* 1959, 66, 297-333.

178. WILSON, C. *The Stature of Man.* Houghton, 1959.

179. WILSON, F. Human nature and esthetic growth, *in* Moustakas, C. (ed.). *The Self.* Harper, 1956.

180. Unpublished manuscripts on Art Education.

181. WINTHROP, H. Some neglected considerations concerning the problems of value in psychology, *J. of General Psychol.,* 1961, 64, 37-59.

182. Some aspects of value in psychology and psychiatry, *Psychological Record,* 1961, 11, 119-132.

183. WOODGER, J. *Biological Principles.* Harcourt, 1929.

184. WOODWORTH, R. *Dynamics of Behavior.* Holt, 1958.

185. YOUNG, P. T. *Motivation and Emotion.* Wiley, 1961.

186. ZUGER, B. Growth of the individuals concept of self. A.M.A. Amer. *J. Diseased Children,* 1952, 83, 719.

187. The states of being and awareness in neurosis and their redirection in therapy, *J. of Nervous and Mental Disease,* 1955, 121, 573.

Footnotes:

[¹ "But paradoxically, the art experience cannot be effectively *used* for this purpose or any other. It must be a purposeless activity, as far as we understand 'purpose'. It can only be an experience in *being*—being a human organism doing what it must and what it is privileged to do—experiencing life keenly and wholly, expending energy and creating beauty in its own style—and the increased sensitivity, integrity, efficiency, and feeling of well-being are by-products" (179, p. 213).]

[² "From the moment the package is in his hands, he feels free to do what he wants with it. He opens it, speculates on what it is, recognizes what it is, expresses happiness or disappointment, notices the arrangement of the contents, finds a book of directions, feels the touch of the steel, the different weights of the parts, and their number, and so on. He does all this before he has attempted to do a thing with the set. Then comes the thrill of doing something with it. It may be only matching one single part with another. Thereby alone he gets a feeling of having done something, that he can do something, and that he is not helpless with that particular article. Whatever pattern is subsequently followed, whether his interest extends to the full utilization of the set and therefore toward further gaining a feeling of greater and greater accomplishment, or whether he completely discards it, his initial contact with the erector set has been meaningful.

"The results of active experiencing can be summarized approximately in the following way. There is physical, emotional, and intellectual self-involvement; there is a recognition and further exploration of one's abilities; there is initiation of activity or creativeness; there is finding out one's own pace and rhythm and the assumption of enough of a task for one's abilities at that particular time, which would include the avoidance of taking on too much; there is gain in skill which one can apply to other enterprises, and there is an opportunity each time that one has an active part in something, no matter how small, to find out more and more what one is interested in.

"The above situation may be contrasted with another in which the person who brings home the erector set says to the child, 'Here is an erector set, let me open it for you.' He does so, and then points out all the things in the box, the book of directions, the various parts, etc., and, to top it off, he sets about building one of the complicated models, let us say, a crane. The child may be much interested in what he has seen being done, but let us focus on one aspect of what has really been happening. The child has had no opportunity to get himself involved with the erector set, with his body, his intelligence, or his feelings, he has had no opportunity to match himself up with something that is new for him, to find out what he is capable of or to gain further direction for his interests. The building of the crane for him may have brought in another factor. It may have left the child with an implied demand that he do likewise without his having had an opportunity to prepare himself for any such complicated task. The end becomes the object instead of the experience involved in the process of attaining the objective. Also, whatever he may subsequently do by himself will look small and mean compared to what had been made for him by someone else. He has not added to his total experience for coming up against something new for the next time. In other words, he has not grown from within but has had something superimposed from the outside. . . . Each bit of active experiencing is an opportunity toward finding out what he likes or dislikes, and more and more what he wants to make out of himself. It is an essential part of his progress toward the stage of maturity and self-direction" (186, p. 179).]

[³ "How is it possible to lose a self? The treachery, unknown and unthinkable, begins with our secret psychic death in childhood—if and when we are not loved and are cut off from our spontaneous wishes. (Think: what is left?) But wait—victim might even "outgrow" it—but it is a perfect double crime in which he him-it is not just this simple murder of a psyche. That might be written off, the tiny self also gradually and unwittingly takes part. He has not been accepted for himself, as *he is*." Oh, they love' him, but they want him or force him or expect him to be different! Therefore he *must be unacceptable*. He himself learns to believe it and at last even takes it for granted. He has truly given himself up. No matter now whether he obeys them, whether he clings, rebels or withdraws—his behavior, his performance is all that matters. His center of gravity is in 'them,' not in himself—yet if he so much as noticed it he'd think it natural enough. And the whole thing is entirely plausible; all invisible, automatic, and anonymous!

"This is the perfect paradox. Everything looks normal; ne crime was intended; there is no corpse, no guilt. All we can see is the sun rising and setting as usual. But what has happened? He has been rejected, not only by them, but by himself. (He is actually without a self.) What has he lost? Just the one true and vital part of himself: his own yes-feeling, which is his very capacity for growth, his root system. But alas, he is not dead. 'Life' goes on, and so must he. From the moment he gives himself up, and to the extent that he does so, all unknowingly he sets about to create and maintain a pseudo-self. But this is an expediency—a 'self without wishes. This one shall be loved (or feared) where he is despised, strong where he is weak; it shall go through the motions (oh, but they are caricatures!) not for fun or joy but for survival; not simply because it wants to move but because it has to obey. This necessity is not life—not his life—it is a defense mechanism against death. It is also the machine of death. From now on he will be torn apart by compulsive (unconscious) *needs* or ground by (unconscious) conflicts into paralysis, every motion and every instant canceling out his being, his integrity; and all the while he is disguised as a normal person and expected to behave like one!

"In a word, I saw that we *become* neurotic seeking or defending a pseudo-self, a self-system; and we *are* neurotic to the extent that we are self-less" (7, p. 3).]

[⁴ I think it is possible to apply this general principle to Freudian theory of the progression of libidinal stages. The infant in the oral stage, gets most of his delights through the mouth. And one in particular which has been neglected is that of mastery. We should remember that the *only* thing an infant can do well and efficiently is to suckle. In all else he is inefficient, incapable and if, as I think, this is the earliest precursor of self esteem (feeling of mastery), then this is the *only* way in which the infant can experience the delight of mastery (efficiency, control, self expression, volition.)

But soon he develops other capacities for mastery and control. I mean here not only anal control which though correct, has, in my opinion, been overplayed. Motility and sensory capacities also develop enough during the so-called "anal" stage to give feelings of delight and mastery. But what is important for us here is that the oral infant tends to play out his oral mastery and to become bored with it, just as he becomes bored with milk alone. In a free choice situation, he tends to give up the breast and milk in favor of the more complex activities and tastes, or anyway, to add to the breast these other "higher" developments.

Given sufficient gratification, free choice and lack of threat, he "grows" out of the oral stage and renounces it himself. He doesn't have to be "kicked upstairs," or forced on to maturity as is so often implied. He *chooses* to grow on to higher delights, to become bored with older ones. Only under the impact of danger, threat, failure, frustration, or stress does he tend to regress or fixate; only then does he prefer safety to growth. Certainly renunciation, delay in gratification and the ability to withstand frustration are also necessary for strength, and we know that unbridled gratification is dangerous. And yet it remains true that these qualifications are *subsidiary* to the principle that sufficient gratification of basic needs is *sine qua non*.]

[5 A kind of pseudo-growth takes place very commonly when the person tries (by repression, denial, reaction-formation, etc.) to convince himself that an ungratified basic need has really been gratified, or doesn't exist. He then permits himself to grow on to higher-need-levels, which of course, forever after, rest on a very shaky foundation. I call this "pseudo-growth by bypassing the ungratified need." Such a need perseverates forever as an unconscious force (repetition compulsion).]

[6 I made no effort to explore, nor did any of my subjects spontaneously speak of what may be called the "nadir experiences," e.g., the (to some) painful and crushing insights into the inevitability of aging and death, of ultimate aloneness and responsibility of the individual, of the impersonality of nature, of the nature of the unconscious, etc.]

[7 Compare with Coleridge's statement "If a man could pass through Paradise in a dream, and have a flower presented to him as a pledge that his soul had really been there, and if he found that flower in his hand when he awoke—Ay! and what then?" E. Schneider (ed.) *Samuel Taylor Coleridge: Selected Poetry & Prose*, Rinehart, 1951, p. 477.]

[8 This is of special interest to therapists not only because integration is one of the main goals of all therapy, but also because of the fascinating problems involved in what we may call the "therapeutic dissociation." For therapy to occur from insight, it is necessary to experience and to observe simultaneously. For instance, the psychotic who is totally experiencing but not detached enough to observe his experiencing is unimproved by this experiencing, even though he may have been right in the middle of the unconscious that is so hidden to neurotics. But it is also true that the therapist must split in the same paradoxical way, since he must simultaneously accept and not-accept the patient; that is, on the one hand, he must give "unconditional positive regard" (143), he must identify with the patient in order to understand him, he must put aside all criticisms and evaluations, he must experience the patient's Weltanschauung, he must fuse with him in an I-Thou encounter, he must in a broad Agapean sense, love him, etc. And yet, on the other hand, he is also implicitly disapproving, not-accepting, not-identifying, etc. because he is trying to improve him, to make him better than he is, which means something other than he is right now. These therapeutic splits are quite explicitly a basis of therapy for Deutsch and Murphy (38).

But here, too, the therapeutic goal is, as with multiple personalities, to fuse them into an unsplit harmonious unity, both in the patient and in the therapist. One may also describe it as becoming more and more a purely experiencing ego with self-observation always available as a *possibility*, preconsciously perhaps. In the peak-experiences, we become much more purely experiencing egos.]

[⁹ I realize that I am using language which "points" to the experience, i.e., it will communicate meaning only to those who themselves have not repressed, suppressed, denied, rejected or feared their own peak-experiences. It is possible, I believe, to communicate meaningfully with "non-peakers" also, but this is very laborious and lengthy.]

[¹⁰ This meaning can be communicated easily enough, I think, by calling it the total loss of that self-consciousness or self-awareness or self-observation which is normally with us but which we feel to lower in any absorption or interest or concentration or distraction, or being taken "out of ourselves," whether on the high level of peak-experiences, or on the lower level of becoming so interested in a movie or a novel or a football game as to become forgetful of oneself and one's minor pains, one's appearance, one's worries, etc. This is practically always felt as a pleasant state.]

[¹¹This aspect of authentic identity is so important, has so many overtones, and is so difficult to describe and communicate, that I append the following partial synonyms with their slightly overlapping meanings. Unintentional, of its own accord, free, unforced, unreasoning, undeliberate, impetuous, unreserved, non-withholding, self-disclosing, frank, non-dissembling, open, undissimulating, unpretending, unfeigning, forthright, unsophis ticated, not artificial, unworried, trusting. I leave aside here the question of "innocent cognition," of intuition, B-cognition, etc.]

[¹² "Poetry is the record of the best and happiest moments of the happiest and best minds." P. B. Shelley]

[¹³Probable parallels are perhaps found in the famous Olds experiments (129 a). A white rat, stimulated in the "satisfaction center" of his brain, stops dead, seemingly to "savor" the experience. So also the tendency of human beings having beatific experiences under drugs is to be quiet and nonactive. To hang on to the fading memory of a dream, it is best not to move (69).]

[¹⁴ This tendency to rubricize (instead of using concrete, idiographic, patient-centered experience-language) almost certainly tends to get stronger, even in the very best therapists, when they are ill, tired, preoccupied, anxious, not interested, disrespectful of the patient, in a hurry, etc. It may therefore also serve as an aid in the psychoanalyst's ongoing self-analysis of the countertransference.]

[¹⁵ This thesis can also be read as a contribution to the general problem of communication between therapist and patient. The good therapist faces the task of putting his nomothetic knowledge to idiographic uses. The conceptual framework with which he works and which may be experientially rich and meaningful for him is useless for the patient in its conceptual form. Insight therapy consists not only of uncovering, experiencing, and categorizing unconscious materials. It is also largely a job of pulling together under a concept all sorts of fully conscious but unnamed and therefore unconnected subjective experiences, or even, more simply, giving a name to an unnamed experience. The patient may have the "Aha" experience upon true insight, e.g., "My God! I've really hated my mother all the time that I thought I loved her!" But he may also have it without reference to any unconscious materials, e.g., "So *that's* what you mean by anxiety!" (referring to such and such experiences in the stomach, the throat, the legs, the heart of which he has been perfectly aware but has never named). Such considerations should be helpful also in the training of therapists.]

[16 This is also one way out of the circularity so characteristic of theoretical and semantic discussions of values. For example, this gem from a cartoon: "Good is better than evil because it is nicer."

It is a testable phrasing of Nietzsche's injunction to "Be what thou art," or Kierkegaard's "to be that self which one truly is," or Rogers' "What human beings appear to be striving for, when they are free to choose."]

[17 This word was suggested by Dr. Richard Farson.]

[18 I am not sure how much real difference of opinion there is here. For instance, a passage from Hartmann (p. 92) seems to me to agree with my thesis above, especially in his emphasis on "authentic values."

Compare with the following concise statement by Feuer (43, pp. 13-14): "The distinction between *authentic* values and *inauthentic* ones is one between values which are *expressive* of the primal drives of the organism and those which are *anxiety-induced*. It is the contrast between values which are expressive of the free personality and those which are repressive through fear and taboo. This is the distinction which is at the basis of ethical theory, and the development of an applied social science for the working out of men's happiness."]

[19 The word "transcendence" is used for lack of better. "Independence of" implies too simple a dichotomizing of self and of environment, and therefore is incorrect. "Transcendence" unfortunately implies for some a "higher" which spurns and repudiates the "lower," i.e., again a false dichotomizing. In other contexts I have used as a contrast with "dichotomous way of thinking," the hierarchical-integrative way of thinking, which implies simply that the higher is built upon, rests upon but includes the lower. For instance the central nervous system or the hierarchy of basic needs or an army is hierarchically integrated. I use the word "transcendence" here in the hierarchical-integrative sense rather than in the dichotomous sense.]

[20 Examples of this kind of transcendence are Walt Whitman or William James who were profoundly American, most *purely* American, and yet were also very purely supra-cultural, internationalist members of the whole human species. They were universal men not in *spite* of their being Americans, but just *because* they were such good Americans. So too, Martin Buber, a Jewish philosopher, was *also* more than Jewish. Hokusai, profoundly Japanese, was a universal artist. Probably *any* universal art cannot be rootless. *Merely* regional art is different from the regionally rooted art that becomes broadly general— human. We may remind ourselves here also of Piaget's children who could not conceive of being simultaneously Genevan and Swiss until they matured to the point of being able to include one within the other and both simultaneously in a hierarchically-integrated way. This and other examples are given by Allport (3).]

[21 These informal remarks were delivered before reading a formal paper before a Karen Horney Memorial meeting of the Association for the Advancement of Psychoanalysis, October 5, 1960. They are included here just about as spoken because they are appropriate to this section on "Future Tasks."]

[22 For instance, I feel that everything I am trying to express here is far better expressed by Saul Steinberg in his amazing: series of sketches in the *New Yorker* during the last year. In these "existential cartoons," this fine artist has used not a single word. But think how they would fit in the bibliography of a "serious" paper in a "serious" journal, or, for that matter, on the program of this conference, even though its subject matter and his are the same, i.e., Identity and Alienation.]

CPSIA information can be obtained at www.ICGtesting.com
Printed in the USA
LVOW040500210712

290855LV00002B/163/P

9 781617 202667